The Very Best of
KwaZulu-Natal

Sue Derwent

The Very Best of
KwaZulu-Natal

Sue Derwent

Struik Publishers (Pty) Ltd
(a member of Struik New Holland Publishing (Pty) Ltd)
80 McKenzie Street, Cape Town 8001
Reg. No.: 54/00965/07

London • Cape Town • Sydney • Auckland
24 Nutford Place, London W1H 6DQ, United Kingdom
80 McKenzie Street, Cape Town 8001
3/2 Aquatic Drive, Frenchs Forest, NSW 2086, Australia
218 Lake Road, Northcote, Auckland, New Zealand

ISBN 1 86872 415 8

First published in 2000

2 4 6 8 10 9 7 5 3 1

Publishing manager: Annlerie van Rooyen
Managing editor: Lesley Hay-Whitton
Editors: Glynne Newlands and Inge du Plessis
Designer: Tracey Mackenzie
Cartographer: John Loubser
Picture researcher: Carmen Watts
Proofreader and Indexer: Sandie Vahl
Reproduction: Hirt & Carter Cape (Pty) Ltd
Printed and bound by Times Offset (M) Sdn Bhd

FRONT COVER *Durban's beachfront at dusk.*
BACK COVER *The Amphitheatre in the Royal Natal National Park forms an impressive backdrop to the lower-lying farmlands.*
SPINE *A young Zulu woman dressed in traditional attire, at Dumazulu cultural village near Hluhluwe.*
HALF TITLE PAGE *Zulu maidens adorned with colourful, beaded apparel relax at Shaka's Kraal, a cultural village in Zululand.*
TITLE PAGES *The magnificent Cathedral Peak in the Drakensberg mountains.*
THIS PAGE *Sunrise at Bhanga Nek beach, north of Sodwana Bay.*
PAGE 6 *A well-camouflaged scorpionfish on a coral reef at Aliwal Shoal, which lies off the coast between Umkomaas and Scottburgh.*
PAGE 8–9 *Third Lake – one of four freshwater lakes at Kosi Bay – is home to crocodiles, hippos and a variety of fish.*
PAGE 144 *The once-endangered white rhino is now a common sight at the Hluhluwe-Umfolozi Park.*

AUTHOR'S ACKNOWLEDGEMENTS
I would like to thank Craig Daniels for his generosity and hospitality; Lee
Martins for the loan of her cottage at Kei Mouth while I was writing the book;
editors Glynne Newlands and Inge du Plessis (it was such a pleasure working
with you), and the rest of the Struik team. I am also grateful to the people at
Phinda Resource Reserve, Tembe Safari Camp, KwaZulu-Natal Conservation
Services, Isandlwana Lodge, and in particular Andy Coetzee at Rocktail Bay
Lodge and Paul Ross at Ardmore. Finally, I would like to thank my family
and all my friends and colleagues who have assisted me with information,
accommodation and good humour.

CONTENTS

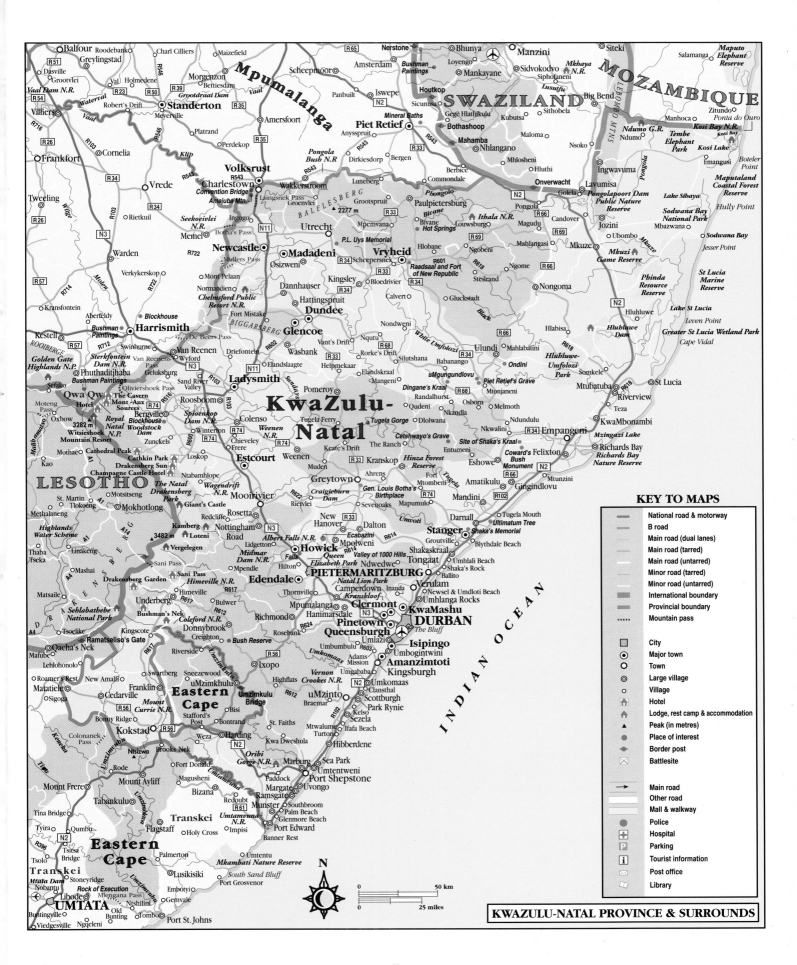

KEY TO MAPS

———	National road & motorway
———	B road
———	Main road (dual lanes)
———	Main road (tarred)
———	Main road (untarred)
———	Minor road (tarred)
———	Minor road (untarred)
	International boundary
	Provincial boundary
·····	Mountain pass
▢	City
◉	Major town
○	Town
◎	Large village
○	Village
⌂	Hotel
⌂	Lodge, rest camp & accommodation
▲	Peak (in metres)
●	Place of interest
⬩	Border post
⊠	Battlesite
→	Main road
	Other road
	Mall & walkway
●	Police
✚	Hospital
P	Parking
i	Tourist information
✉	Post office
📖	Library

KWAZULU-NATAL PROVINCE & SURROUNDS

$\mathcal{P}$erhaps more than any other of South Africa's nine provinces, KwaZulu-Natal encapsulates the feel of contemporary Africa. Modern sophistication mixes with old traditional rituals, and while wild animals range through some of the country's most famous game reserves and mighty raptors soar above the majestic Drakensberg mountains, the descendants of British, Boer, Indian and other settlers from distant countries reside in a bustle of vibrant urban centres alongside the Zulu people, from whom the province derives part of its name.

Before South Africa's first historic democratic elections in 1994, the province was known by the colonial name Natal, which it received from Portuguese explorer Vasco da Gama. So impressed was he with the beauty of the coastline when he first caught sight of it on Christmas day in 1947 that he called it *Terra de Natalia*. However, after 1994, the nominally independent homeland of KwaZulu, which had been created by the apartheid government, joined the rest of the province which then became known as KwaZulu-Natal. *eZulweni*, from which the name 'Zulu' is derived, means 'heaven', an apt name for a province which is well known for its glorious subtropical climate, some of the country's finest game reserves, its brooding mountain ranges, and its wonderful beaches, stretching 480 kilometres from the Wild Coast of the Eastern Cape to the border of Mozambique.

The Very Best of KwaZulu-Natal offers an insight into some of the better-known places in the province, as well as the most fascinating. Durban is South Africa's third-largest city and the busiest port in the country, and it is here that the visitor will experience an African city in transition. Pietermaritzburg, which shares its status as capital city of KwaZulu-Natal with Ulundi, has a more gentle pace and many reminders, both architectural

and cultural, of the province's colonial past. The Drakensberg forms a barrier between Lesotho and the lower-lying hills of the Midlands, which run down to the coastal plain.

The coastal region south of Durban tends to be more built up than the North Coast, which is less marred by commercial development – the further north you travel along the coast, the more likely you are to experience true African wilderness. Much of the coastline north of the thriving harbour town of Richards Bay is protected, offering a landscape of deserted beaches, towering dunes and virgin coastal forests. Inland is the traditional home of the Zulu people, and sites of the Anglo-Boer and Anglo-Zulu wars. It is here, too, that you will be able to visit KwaZulu-Natal's wonderful game reserves which easily rival the country's famous Kruger National Park, if not in size, then definitely in atmosphere and their diversity of plants and animals.

Although the cities and towns of the province offer an excitement of cultural, shopping and sporting activities, they are always close to traditional Africa. From the call to prayer by muezzin in their urban minarets and the hectic hooting of the mini-bus taxis, it is only a short distance to hear the low whistle of cattle herders and feel the wind whispering through the long grass and lonely graves of the now silent battlefields. The wistful cry of the fish eagle and the cerulean waves sighing onto the beaches are never far away from urban sophistication.

KwaZulu-Natal is a destination that continues to intrigue, challenge and excite both visitors and locals alike, because no matter how much time you spend here, there is always so much more to see and experience.

Sue Derwent

Durban –
Bay City

LEFT *The warm waters of the Indian Ocean wash the shores of Durban, drawing visitors to this sunny and friendly holiday city. A range of hotels overlooks the central swimming beaches, which are enjoyed by pedestrians, bathers and surfers alike.*

ABOVE *Dolphins can often be seen playing in the waves along KwaZulu-Natal's coastline. It is possible to see them close up at Seaworld's Dolphinarium (see page 19).*

Durban – Bay City

The Golden Mile • The Harbour Area • City Centre • Indian Town • Across the Berea
Northern Durban • Western Durban • South-Central

Durban is a city of sweltering summer days, massive trees dripping with humidity, and the heady smells of aromatic spices, exhaust fumes, suntan lotion and sea breezes off the warm Indian Ocean. Although geographically it may not be the centre of KwaZulu-Natal, it is certainly the hub, as diverse masses of people bump and hustle through the city. Durban is not big by international standards (its population is about 3.2 million), even though it sprawls north-, west- and southwards, coming to an end at the edge of the Indian Ocean.

This is an African city in the true sense of the word, a city of contrasts. Expensive hotels and guest houses grace the beachfront, while noisy vendors sell their wares on many of the streets. Art collections adorn the walls of sophisticated galleries, while outside mini-bus taxis hoot and jostle in the traffic. Western-style hospitals and traditional African healers both attend to all sorts of ailments. And within 30 minutes of watching thousands of people pouring out onto a busy central city railway station, or an enormous tanker dock in Durban's bustling port, or smelling acrid exhaust fumes off the hot tar streets, you could be in the deepest of rural Africa watching small Zulu boys herding cattle or viewing wild game tentatively approaching a water hole to drink.

Durban's safe harbour, tucked in the arm of the Bluff, was one of the main reasons for the city's development, and it has since become one of Africa's busiest ports, serving the vast southern African interior. However, the bay is not just about trade and commerce. On a warm and breezy day, boardsailers, yachts in full sail, and canoeists can be spotted amongst the massive tankers and cargo ships as they are guided in and out of the harbour by the little black and white tugs and pilot boats.

Because of its subtropical climate, warm seas and safe swimming beaches, Durban has always been a holiday city, drawing visitors from all over. Even in winter, one seldom needs a warm jersey, except maybe in the evenings. It is not surprising, then, that leisure activities are focused either on the sea or the climate.

But it is perhaps Durban's cultural diversity that gives it the richness and vibrancy enjoyed by few other South African cities. By far the largest section of Durban's population is Zulu-speaking, and evidence of their culture is everywhere – in the markets, in the art galleries and theatres, on the streets, and in the sprawling townships that surround the city. The Indian population have also brought their colourful food, rituals and ceremonies to enrich Durban, while evidence of the European settlers can also be seen throughout the city.

ABOVE *Indian cuisine is a hot favourite in the city. A variety of exotic, aromatic spices can be purchased at the vibrant Victoria Street Market, which lies to the west of the city centre (see page 32).*

OPPOSITE *Once a formal part of Durban's transport system, the ricksha men with their elaborate head-dresses are now a tourist attraction, transporting visitors along the Golden Mile (see page 18).*

THE GOLDEN MILE

⬇ The Bluff

⬅ Addington Hospital

⬅ The Point

⬇ Trampolines and Little Top

⬇ The Lido

Ricksha Men

Wedge Beach

⬇ Dolphinarium

⬇ Seaworld

⬆ Old West Street Jetty

Dairy Beach

Paddling Pools and Amusement Park ⬆

Indian Ocean

⬇ Dairy Beach Pier

North Beach

⬇ Brighton Beach

John Ross House with Revolving Restaurant ➡

The Harbour (*see* page 21)

⬇ Victoria Park

⬇ Ocean Sports Centre

⬇ Rachel Findlayson Pool

THE GOLDEN MILE

Durban's beaches have always been one of its premier tourist attractions. The 6-kilometre-long stretch of beachfront, where the city meets the ocean, is known as the Golden Mile and is one of Durban's most popular recreational areas. The Golden Mile is divided into the northern section, with beaches such as Blue Lagoon, Tekweni, Battery Beach and Laguna; the central beaches comprising the Bay of Plenty, North Beach (strangely enough), Dairy and Wedge beaches; and the southern beaches, made up of South Beach, Addington and Vetch's Beach.

Fitzsimons Snake Park and Minitown, a miniature reconstruction of Durban, complete with hotels, airport and harbour, are situated between Battery Beach and the Bay of Plenty.

The central section of the Golden Mile is bounded by high-rise hotels, amusement centres, restaurants, gardens, paddling pools, and a long promenade used extensively by the city's local 'baggies and board brigade'. As no cars are allowed along this promenade, it is popular with casual evening and early-morning strollers, and is almost always abuzz with activity as surfers, cyclists, joggers, roller-bladers and anglers enjoy everything the beachfront has to offer. Sunday mornings see the Golden Mile filled with families enjoying a day at the beach, or a hearty brunch at **The Deck, Joe Cools** or any one of the many promenade restaurants.

A number of pedestrian piers jut out into the rolling waves, giving strollers a vantage point from which to watch the surfers and body-boarders. Most of KwaZulu-Natal's beaches are protected by shark nets and staffed with lifeguards. The nets were installed by the Sharks Board (*see* page 39) in 1952, making these beaches among the safest on the South African coast.

Waterworld

Waterworld, just north of Battery Beach, is a fun alternative to a day on the beach. It boasts enormous two-storey waterslides, pools and other opportunities to enjoy a variety of gentle, pulsating or looping water-propelled rides. Tired parents can relax on the ample grassy lawns.

Fitzsimons Snake Park

At the northern end of the Golden Mile lies the Fitzsimons Snake Park. Here, demonstrations and talks are given daily during holiday seasons, with snake feeding taking place regularly. Demonstrations of 'milking' the poison from some of the venomous snakes are also given. While the emphasis is on indigenous snakes, such as mambas, pythons and adders, there is also a number of other creepy-crawlies to view – tortoises, lizards and frogs, for example – and thermostatically controlled cages house a variety of exotic snakes. The staff are knowledgeable and friendly and have a host of interesting tales to tell, such as the time they were brought a two-headed snake, which sadly did not survive very long.

Amphitheatre Gardens

On Sundays, the Amphitheatre Gardens off North Beach host an enormous **flea market** which overlooks the Indian Ocean – if you can catch a glimpse of it through the crowds. Locally made traditional African crafts vie for space among cheap and garish plastic goods made in China, India and the Philippines, second-hand books sit alongside hand-crafted leatherwork, and the aromas of samoosas and candyfloss pervade. During the rest of the week, this sunken garden with its subtropical flowers, fish ponds and fountains forms a pleasant green and grassy retreat between some of the big hotels and the promenade and beach.

OPPOSITE *The paddling pools and amusement park along the Golden Mile are ideal for children when the sea is a little rough.*

ABOVE *Shooting down Waterworld's wet wonderland of slides is a favourite among children and adults alike.*

LEFT *Bobbing around in a big tube at Waterworld is a great way to cool down during the hot summer holidays.*

Beadwork and Basket Sellers

The entrepreneurial spirit of the informal traders is evident along the Golden Mile. Here, basket and beadwork sellers add another dimension of colour to the beachfront area. Many of the women make their craftwork on the spot and it is fascinating to watch long, thin strips of reed and grass being transformed into a colourful basket before your eyes.

Most of these handicraft sellers are the sole breadwinners in their families and many belong to the Nazareth Baptist Church. Their prophet, Shembe, was a strong advocate of self-employment, believing that dependence on others for one's livelihood was undesirable and that people should cultivate and sell fresh produce or embark on craft-making enterprises to earn their living (*see* page 40, Ebuhleni). The prices of these crafts are generally most reasonable and visitors are encouraged to support these entrepreneurs in making a living, while at the same time helping to keep traditional crafts alive.

Ricksha Men

For many people, ricksha men are synonymous with the city of Durban as nowhere else in South Africa will you be able to enjoy a ricksha ride.

Rickshas were first introduced to the city in 1893 as a means of transport for both goods and people. At one stage there were more than 2 000 ricksha pullers but, today, since they are now mainly a tourist attraction along the beachfront, there are only 20 or so registered ricksha men left.

The flamboyant costumes that are worn by these Zulu men developed as a result of rivalry among the pullers, and are fascinating to see (*see* the photograph on page 13). The headgear often consist of massive beaded cow horns, mirrors, feathers and skins, and it takes some skill for these ricksha men to balance their headgear and perform their antics while treating tourists to a ride along the promenade in their gaily decorated carts.

Seaworld, Dolphinarium and Oceanographic Research Institute

Towards the centre of the Golden Mile lies the Oceanographic Research Institute, attached to which is Seaworld and the Dolphinarium. Dolphin, seal and penguin shows take place daily at the Dolphinarium, delighting children and adults alike, while one of the main attractions of Seaworld is the shark tank.

In its aquarium, scuba divers regularly feed the giant sea turtles, stingrays and other fish by hand, a rather awesome sight to see. The Oceanographic Research Institute has played a significant role in the conservation of marine life along South Africa's coastline and is involved in a number of highly acclaimed research projects on the breeding and protection of fish and other marine resources.

OPPOSITE *Anna Buthelezi, along with many other Zulu women, sells her beadwork, pottery and basketry along the Golden Mile, keeping traditional crafts alive.*

ABOVE *Pigeons gather on the promenade in front of Seaworld and the Dolphinarium, waiting to be chased by happy children or to be fed by passing pedestrians as they take a stroll along the Golden Mile.*

RIGHT *A close encounter with dolphins at Seaworld's Dolphinarium is a highlight for many children at the daily dolphin shows.*

The Ocean Action Festival

The Ocean Action Festival, which includes the world-famous **Gunston 500 Surf Competition** – one of the longest-running surf competitions in the world – takes place along the Golden Mile during Durban's winter months. During this popular event, the promenade is transformed into an exciting carnival, with stalls selling anything from sunglasses and wetsuits to spicy pineapples on a stick. What started as a fairly ordinary local competition over 30 years ago has become a major event on the international surfing calendar. With the introduction of the Ocean Action Festival in 1992, the competition has evolved into a feast of sports such as body-boarding, jetskiing and the gruelling iron-man competition, and beach events such as volleyball, kick-boxing and street soccer.

One of the highlights of the festival is the somewhat controversial night surfing event. It has drawn criticism in some circles because it is believed that the high-powered spotlights could attract sharks into the area. Be that as it may, the event is spectacular to watch and is enjoyed by surfers and spectators alike.

The winter swell draws surfers in their hundreds to take part in the internationally famous Gunston 500 Surf Competition.

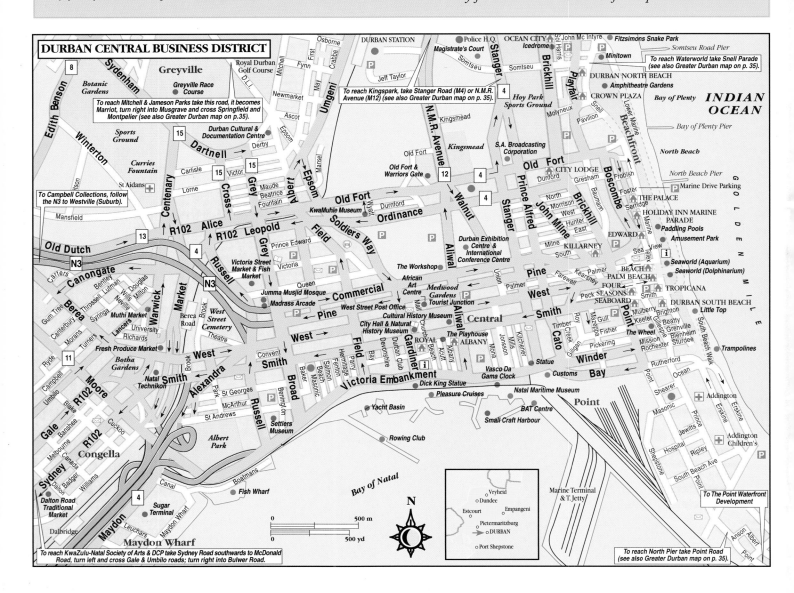

THE HARBOUR

Indian Ocean

Vetch's Beach ⬇

The Bluff ➡

The Point ➡

Da Gama Clock ⬇

⬇ BAT Centre

⬅ Small Craft Harbour

⬆ Maritime Museum

Dick King Statue ⬇

⬇ Pleasure Cruises

Point Yacht Club

Royal Natal Yacht Club

Victoria Embankment

To Sugar Terminal ➡

THE HARBOUR AREA

At the far southern end of the Golden Mile, the recreational beaches come to an end at the harbour mouth. From North Pier, the docks sweep around in a curve edging onto the city along the Esplanade (or Victoria Embankment). This is a favourite recreational space for Durban's residents because it is from along the harbour's edge that you can see massive ships move in and out of the busy port, watch graceful yachts and dingy sailboats bobbing around in the water, or on breezy days the windsurfers racing backwards and forwards among the

OPPOSITE Yachts of all shapes and sizes, from all parts of the world, bob gently in their safe mooring in the yacht basin on the western edge of the harbour.

BELOW The city's high-rise offices and apartment blocks enjoy a spectacular view over the bay with its busy little tugs guiding ships in and out of the harbour.

other water craft. At sunset or in the evenings, canoeists can often be seen paddling across the bay from the yacht basin. There are a number of restaurants with lovely views of the bay and the working harbour, and it is a delight to enjoy a meal at night with the city lights twinkling in the water.

The *Harbour Ferry*

A really enjoyable way to experience the harbour is to take a trip on the *Harbour Ferry*. Although there are commercial ferries, charter boats and pleasure cruises, such as the *Sarie Marais*, *Isle of Capri* and the *African Queen*, which take tours of the harbour and are perhaps more informative (and expensive), the *Harbour Ferry* is a working ferry and taking a trip on it is an exciting way to meet the locals and see life from a different perspective. It transports harbour workers around the docks, fishermen out to the South Pier, sailors from anchorage to the city, sex-workers from the city to the ships, and, of course, the more adventurous visitor on an authentic tour of the harbour.

and drink while watching dolphin and fish playing and feeding under the spotlights.

Plans are afoot to develop this area, generally known as The Point, into a major tourist attraction. Future proposals include an underwater museum and auditorium, an entertainment dome with virtual-reality features, a three-storey shopping complex, a museum, recording studios, jazz clubs, coffee shops and a maze of stalls and shops catering for local and international tourists. At the time of writing, a variety of restaurants, live entertainment venues, rows of beautifully restored terraced cottages and a flea market at the actual point were already on offer. Other venues of interest can also be enjoyed around the bay's edge.

BAT Centre

From across the Bay, the Bartle Arts Trust (BAT) Centre resembles an enormous bat in flight. The BAT, as it is affectionately known, was established in 1995 and is administered by a charitable trust which aims to support and celebrate the province's rich cultural heritage. Painters, sculptors, dancers and musicians work in the various studios and galleries, and there are also regular dance, art and music workshops and writing classes. At night the BAT comes alive with local theatre productions, African film or video festivals and live music.

The Point Waterfront

North Pier guards the harbour mouth, and it is from this point southwards around the quayside that Durban's fledgling Point Waterfront begins. At any time of the day or night, North Pier is usually packed with ever-hopeful anglers, patiently casting their fishing lines into the ocean.

Along the quayside are a number of restaurants from where you can sit and watch massive ships moving in and out of this busy port. A popular watering hole on hot and sultry Durban nights is **Thirsty's,** a favourite place with locals who come to eat

The **Open Window Network (OWN)**, also housed in the BAT Centre, promotes developing community television and provides a production training resource facility for community organisations, as well as for individuals interested in film and

video. Downstairs are shops and galleries showcasing South African crafts, and a **news café**, a great place to sit and watch people, read the daily papers, eat muffins and drink tea. Upstairs, a **small bar** opens onto a wide veranda overlooking the harbour, a wonderful vantage point from which to watch the tug-boats chuffing backwards and forwards while enjoying a sundowner.

Port Natal Maritime Museum

Close to the BAT Centre is the Maritime Museum. Durban used to be known as Port Natal, and the museum is a reminder of Durban harbour's origins and its subsequent development into the busiest port in southern Africa. The three large exhibits which make up the museum consist of an old 1927 steam-tug, the *Ulundi*, the 1961 twin-screw, oil-fired steam-tug *JR More*, and the 1957 minesweeper *SAS Durban*. At certain times of the day, a fascinating audio-visual about pirates is shown.

Vasco da Gama Clock

The beautifully ornate Vasco da Gama Clock on the Victoria Embankment commemorates the Portuguese explorer who, on first sighting the lovely coastline on Christmas eve 1497, called it *Terra de Natalia*, from which the province took its name. The clock was originally installed in Point Road in 1897, just over 400 years after this event. A small stone plaque lies next to the clock, which was unveiled in 1969 by the Portuguese ambassador on the 500th anniversary of Da Gama's birth.

Dick King Statue

In 1842, a young man of about 17 years of age, thought to have been accompanied by his 16-year-old servant, Ndongeni, rode a gruelling 970 kilometres from Port Natal to Grahamstown in just 10 days. Their mission was to obtain assistance for the British troops who were, at the time, besieged by the Boers in Durban's Old Fort. Today, there is a large statue of young Dick King on the corner of Gardiner Street and the Victoria Embankment, and two bronze plaques commemorate the heroic ride. Dick King was a hunter and trader and apparently had a shop a short way from the Market Square (today's Farewell Square). A plaque marks this site at the corner of Smith and Dick King streets, which lie east of Aliwal Street.

OPPOSITE TOP *North Pier, which protects the entrance to the harbour, is a favourite spot among anglers.*

OPPOSITE BOTTOM LEFT *Patrons at the waterfront eateries can enjoy a good meal while watching the activities of the bay.*

OPPOSITE BOTTOM RIGHT *The BAT Centre is a cultural home to visual and performing artists from all sectors of the city and its surroundings.*

ABOVE *Interesting maritime relics can be seen at the Maritime Museum.*

FAR LEFT *The beautifully ornate Da Gama Clock commemorates the Portuguese voyager, Vasco da Gama, who gave the province its first colonial name – Natal.*

LEFT *Dick King, one of Durban's courageous young men, is remembered for his heroic ride to obtain assistance for the besieged British troops in 1842.*

The Yacht Basin and Small Craft Harbour

The yacht basin, a little further down the bay, is a wonderful place to wander around and watch the 'yachties' pottering about on their boats. For those who tire of walking, but would still like to observe all the bayside activities, **Café Fish**, with its elegant glass architecture poised just over the water's edge, is a superb place to sit and enjoy a snack or a sundowner as the sun slips away behind the tall buildings along the palm-lined Victoria Embankment, and the city lights shimmer in the water. Another spot from which to enjoy the bay is **Charlie Croft's**, in the Small Craft Harbour, where, instead of watching recreational sailors, you can see boat-builders at work.

Sugar Terminal

Much of Durban's early economy was built on the sugar industry, and even today the hills and fields around the city and along the north and south coasts are covered in sugar cane. It is not surprising, then, that Durban's Sugar Terminal is the largest in southern Africa and one of the most advanced in the world.

A tour around the terminal is informative, as well as a delight of sensual and aromatic experiences. The thick smell of molasses pervades everything and it is extraordinary to see the terminal's three enormous silos, the largest of which is the size of two rugby fields, piled high to the domed ceiling with tons of crunchy raw sugar. The architectural design of the silos has been patented and used in other parts of the world.

CITY CENTRE

Durban's central business district has changed radically in recent years as has its character. Street vendors have laid claim to large parts of the central areas, transforming Durban into a noisy, colourful African city. Although it is still home to some of the larger chain stores and is as busy as ever, many people prefer to do their shopping in the big shopping malls and complexes that have sprung up around the outskirts of the city.

Tourist Junction

This is a good place from which to start any tour of Durban, as it is placed right in the centre of the city. Tourist Junction is a beautiful old building and was once the administration block of Durban's old Central Railway Station. Today, it houses the offices of **Durban Africa** and **KwaZulu-Natal Tourism**, the booking and information office of the **KwaZulu-Natal Nature Conservation Service**, and the **African Art Centre**, as the central station has been moved slightly north of the city centre. It also houses **Hambe Kahle Tours**, which runs some of the most interesting and well-organised township tours in Durban.

Other walking tours which are run from Tourist Junction include the Oriental Walkabout, the Durban Experience and the Historical Walkabout.

___

OPPOSITE TOP *Water laps gently against the boats in the Small Craft Harbour off Victoria Embankment, reflecting the twinkling lights of the city as the sun goes down.*

OPPOSITE BOTTOM *Mountains of sugary granules pile high inside the busy Sugar Terminal, awaiting shipment to different parts of the world.*

TOP *Traditional healers buy the plants, roots and bark they use to make medicine from street traders, who also sell prepared potions to the general public. (Durban has the biggest* muthi *market in Africa, see page 32.)*

RIGHT *Colourful and detailed wall murals, such as the 'Wall of Peace', brighten the surroundings of the old jail in Old Fort Road and many other buildings in and around the city.*

African Art Centre

The African Art Centre has established itself as a place where traditional and contemporary artworks of quality can be purchased, and is a must for anyone interested in authentic indigenous African art, both contemporary and historic. The centre, which is in the same building as Tourist Junction, promotes local up-and-coming as well as more established African artists, and on sale are original works of art including beadwork, basketry, weaving, ceramics, carving and sculpture from the Zulu and Xhosa cultures. Original works of high quality can be purchased at prices ranging from R3 to R3 000, and there is almost always someone who can tell you more about the artists, their development and the works you may wish to purchase, lending a nice personal touch.

General Post Office and City Hall

Durban's Post Office in West Street was the city's first town hall (completed in 1855), and, although in more recent times it has been extended extensively at the rear, it remains one of South Africa's finest classical buildings. Originally, it housed a postal agency and a museum, and it only became the General Post Office once the present City Hall (across the road between Smith and West streets) was completed in 1910.

The City Hall was built in Edwardian neo-baroque style and today houses the Council Chambers, the Town Clerk's offices, the **Durban Art Gallery,** the **Natural History Museum** and the **General Lending Library.**

Look on the outside of the building to see the allegorical sculptures depicting the Arts, Music and Literature, Commerce and Industry. It is a beautiful building and well worth visiting. Tours can be arranged through Durban Africa, which is based at Tourist Junction.

Natural History Museum

Situated in the City Hall and accessed through a side entrance in Smith Street, this museum is popular with all sectors of the city's population. As you enter the museum you climb up an imposing marble staircase. At the landing on the stairs, you are greeted by an enormous elephant, and at the top of the stairs a tall giraffe towers over the information desk from where you will be guided to a number of galleries.

The P. A. Clancy Gallery houses a collection of birds, including a display of large flightless birds, and the Science Centre consists of a hall of earth sciences dominated by a life-size reconstruction of the dinosaur *Tyrannosaurus rex*. From there, you can experience a 90-second journey through time, with the Human Origins and Evolution display. A very popular gallery is the Kwanunu Insect Arcade. Giant insects adorn the walls, but what grabs the attention, particularly of little boys, is the live specimens of Durban's infamous cockroaches, creeping

and scuttling behind their glass viewing cage. Interestingly, cockroaches are a class of insect that lived at the time of the now extinct dinosaurs.

The museum's amazing displays include Africa's numerous mammals, as well as species of plants, birds and reptiles. If you are not planning to travel to the province's rural areas and game reserves, the Hall of Amphibians and Reptiles may be the closest you will get to seeing Nile crocodiles, lizards, snakes, frogs and turtles.

At the end of your wanderings, rest a while at the museum's coffee shop, **The Waterhole.** It is rather fun to sip your cappuccino sitting in the middle of a 'mangrove swamp'.

Cultural History Museum

Down the road and around the corner in Aliwal Street is the small Cultural History Museum. The first building to be erected on what used to be Durban's Market Square, it was formerly the Court House and the date 1863 marks the Victorian façade of the building. Downstairs is a big circular, well-lit display of fashion in Durban through the ages. Upstairs, behind a wall of glass, are miniature dolls, replicas of important people in Durban's history and development.

Off to the side is a reconstructed haberdashery from Durban's early days, and a wonderful depiction of Francis Farewell's original shack. Farewell was an early settler and trader who set up camp on the site, which is today known as Francis Farewell's Square, in central Durban, just opposite the City Hall. Farewell established a thriving trade in ivory, hippo tusks and buffalo hides with the Zulu King Shaka. Today, a model of Farewell can be found sitting outside his dimly lit wattle and daub structure, in much the same way as he must have done when Durban was still known as Port Natal.

Playhouse Theatre

The romantic old Playhouse Theatre was built during the 1920s in the Tudor revival style. It was taken over by the Natal Performing Arts Council in the 1980s and for decades has continuously provided Durban with entertainment. It has a vibrant Education and Development Department with a busy

programme presenting mobile theatre to schools, providing training and rehearsal space and supporting community arts centres throughout the greater Durban area.

Although the more mainstream theatre and dance productions are performed here, the company's Musical Drama and Dance departments are well known for enthralling productions which portray South African life in a combination of vibrant dance, song and drama. Several venues are found within the Playhouse Complex, but the interior of the main theatre is a delight with its twinkling starlit ceiling and atmosphere of an old Tudor street at night.

International Conference Centre

The presence of the sophisticated, wavy-roofed and elegantly glassed International Conference Centre (ICC) is a testimony to the many contradictions of South Africa and, indeed, KwaZulu-Natal. While on the one hand Durban may be transforming into a typical African city with its informal traders and influx of rural people, on the other hand it also caters for the high-flying national and international corporate business world.

The ICC was designed by local architects and has some of the most sophisticated technology in southern Africa. Together with the adjacent aluminium-clad, high-rise Hilton Hotel, it has placed Durban firmly on the international conference circuit. Already many major conferences have been held at the ICC, drawing visitors from around the world.

OPPOSITE *Night falls over the stately old City Hall as it faces onto Francis Farewell Square with its pleasant green gardens and tall waving palms.*

TOP *The bright bouquets of the flower sellers near the City Hall bring a breath of spring to the city.*

BELOW *Long part of Durban's cultural heritage, the romantic old Playhouse Theatre lends an air of elegance and olde-worlde charm to the city's busy streets.*

The Workshop

Close to the International Conference Centre in the city centre lies The Workshop, once Durban's railway's workshop. The original building was designed with a wonderful harmony which has been retained during the remodelling process which began in 1986. The five massive doors on the south side of the building once allowed trains to enter the cavernous interior. Today, that entrance leads to an exciting variety of up-market shops. The interior still retains its industrial feel with the great metal spans left exposed. Outside there is a small amphitheatre and expansive lawns, at the centre of which is a delightful mosaic fountain designed by Andrew Verster, one of South Africa's leading artists.

KwaMuhle Museum

Not far from the conference centre and Hilton Hotel is the KwaMuhle Museum, housed in what used to be Durban's notorious Department of Native Affairs. This is perhaps ironic considering that the museum today tells the story of the city's apartheid past. Through its powerful displays, the museum provides a fascinating and often heart-breaking look at the misery caused by the laws which reduced the majority of the population to second-class citizens in the country of their birth.

Exhibits provide background to the pass laws, influx control and beerhall systems, and include a particularly interesting permanent exhibit depicting the history of Cato Manor, now a sprawling informal settlement behind the Berea. This area made international news headlines during the race riots and the notorious and barbaric forced removals (the main ones occurred in 1949 and 1959). Today, Cato Manor is the site of one of the most ambitious urban renewal programmes in the

country and can be visited on a township tour (*see* Hamba Kahle Tours, page 45). Many Zulu artefacts which have survived the turbulent past are also displayed, and a **curio shop** sells Zulu art and craftwork and other items of cultural interest.

INDIAN TOWN

Without leaving the city centre, walk a little west of the main shopping area to a place which feels as if it has been transposed from Asia. This vibrant, busy and noisy area, known as Indian Town, includes Grey, Victoria, Queen and Cathedral streets, and is where Indian people set up shop during the apartheid years. Today, Indian Town is still a busy mass of shoppers, noisy taxis, exhaust fume-belching buses, and street vendors selling anything from fruit to traditional African medicine.

Grey Street and the Madrass Arcade

Grey Street is the hub of Indian Town, with its crazy, busy, bazaar atmosphere. Hawkers and street vendors spill off the pavements, and there are shops selling anything from exotic saris, bunny-chows (Durban's famous half loaf of bread filled with curry), cheap plastic goods or expensive sound systems, to curtains and colourful fabrics.

ABOVE *The Workshop, now a busy, modern shopping mall, was once the old workshop of Durban's rail yards.*

OPPOSITE *In the heart of the Indian area, on the corner of Queen and Grey streets, stands the beautifully gold-domed Jumma Musjid Mosque – a spiritual centre to Durban's large Muslim population and a well-known landmark in the city.*

Leading off Grey Street towards the old Emmanuel Cathedral is the historic arcade bazaar known as the Madrass Arcade. This little alley has the atmosphere of India and just about anything your heart desires can be bought within a small radius: combs, radios, sunglasses, African glass beads, brass- and bronzeware, plastic buckets, metal trunks, pencils and little clay Hindu lamps are all for sale. Indian music and the smells of spices and incense fill the air. Here you will be able to delve into yet another aspect of Durban's cultural mosaic.

Jumma Musjid Mosque

Durban is home to the largest mosque in the southern hemisphere, built by Muslims who emigrated to Durban in the nineteenth century. The beautifully domed structure of the Jumma Musjid Mosque, which is sometimes referred to as 'The Grey Street Mosque', dates back to the late 1880s. The mosque has become a feature of Durban's city centre and it is wonderful to hear the characteristic call to prayer over the loud-speakers at various times throughout the day.

Visitors are welcome to visit the mosque, and tours can be arranged of the beautifully refurbished building to learn more about the practices and beliefs of a large part of Durban's population who follow the Islamic faith. Women generally worship at home, although when they do attend mosque, it is in a separate section from the men.

Remember, when visiting the mosque, to ensure that your shoulders are covered, and female visitors should preferably wear a long skirt or dress which covers the legs. However, should you forget, a robe will be provided for you at the entrance. You are also required to leave your shoes outside when entering a mosque.

Durban Cultural and Documentation Centre

The Durban Cultural and Documentation Centre is concerned with the history, culture and development of South Africans of Indian origin, but it also portrays their interaction with other cultures in the country.

The centre serves not only as a place of learning and research, but also provides a venue for the promotion of the visual and performing arts. There are fascinating stories as well as a photographic exhibition about the lives of indentured Indians, and of Mahatma Gandhi's stay in South Africa.

A marvellous, exotic collection of Indian instruments, intricate jewellery, colourful traditional costumes, religious icons, cutlery, farming implements and original documents donated over the years by members of Durban's Indian community is also on display.

If you are planning to visit the centre, it is advisable to call in advance so you can be sure that someone will be available to show you around.

Victoria Street Market and the Fish Market

The original colourful Indian Market burnt down a number of years ago and was replaced by a more modern version. Although it has taken a few years to develop a similar character, the Victoria Street Market is as busy and interesting as its predecessor. The vendors and shopkeepers call and cajole passers-by into their shops and stalls to entice them to buy.

You can purchase just about anything here, from oriental brassware to African baskets, Malawian 'story chairs', Zimbabwean wooden sculptures, Tanzanian masks, Hindu flame lamps, and sacks of lentils and split peas. Cheap plastic curios are displayed alongside small Indian temple bells, and the scent of soaps and sweet-smelling incense mingle with the spicy aromas of curries and spices.

As you step out of the market for a breath of fresh air, you are assailed by exhaust fumes from the mini-bus taxis and the often overpowering smell of fish emanating from the large building right next door. If you can stomach the fishy odours of sea life, such as crabs, squid, crayfish and prawns that arrive fresh from the sea every day, you will find that the Fish Market is every bit as interesting as the Indian Market and that the fishmongers are as colourful and cajoling as their colleagues next door.

Warwick Street Fresh Produce Market

Warwick Street is the venue for a large open-air market selling fresh produce from around the country. The stalls are run mainly by Indian families who have been working there for generations. It is a noisy, colourful, bustling market with vendors calling out, trolleys weaving among the stalls, and shoppers wandering around looking for bargains. The market is walled and usually opens at sunrise. The earlier you get there the better because much of the freshest items are sold early and the bustle of excitement tends to die down in the heat of the day.

Muthi Market

For many years, the pavements around Warwick Street Triangle, across the way from Victoria Street, were crammed with informal traders and traditional healers selling their collections and mixtures of indigenous herbs, plants, bark, snake skins, bird wings, crocodile teeth, dolphin skulls and monkey paws. The area has been upgraded somewhat, and although this may have made it look a little more presentable, much of the atmosphere has been lost. The up-side is that traders, who used to trade directly on the streets, are now housed in more sanitary conditions, and the area is also safer to visit.

This is truly a fascinating market – not only is it the biggest of its kind in the southern hemisphere, but it also gives visitors insight into the beliefs and culture of many black Africans. You may be able to get a *sangoma* (spiritual healer) to 'throw the bones' for you, but many of the people plying their trade here are from rural areas and do not speak English very well. However, there is usually someone around who is willing to act as an interpreter.

The 'stalls' of these informal traders brim with the most amazing-looking concoctions which may appear quite horrifying to a westerner. Their beliefs and traditions may seem alien, but their culture is rich and ancient, and continues to influence much of African life to this day.

Many of Africa's traditional healers have spent years in training and have vast botanical and zoological knowledge, which is increasingly being sought by some of the large pharmaceutical companies.

ACROSS THE BEREA

From the coast, Durban's city bowl area rises slightly onto higher ground, generally referred to as 'the Berea'. This ridge runs from north to south, almost parallel to the coastline. During colonisation, the Berea was one of the first areas to be settled, mainly because it was a little cooler, but also perhaps because of the lovely views afforded across the bay and the sea.

Botanical Gardens

In so many ways Durban's Botanical Gardens retain a feeling of 'old' Durban. Enormous, leafy fig trees shade paths that wind through the lawns and other foliage. Giant cycads cover a

sloping lawn, the lily ponds play host to water birds of all sorts, and mothers and grannies accompany small children on excursions to feed the indigenous ducks and geese.

The first curator of the Botanical Gardens was a Mr Mark Johnson McKen who, from 1850 onwards, painstakingly collected a vast number of plant specimens from all over the world and began introducing them into the garden. The cool, green oasis of fascinating trees and plants provides a quiet, gentle change of pace from the hum of the surrounding city. There is an orchid house, a sunken garden and a herb garden, which contains a number of indigenous herbs still used by African traditional healers, with small signboards explaining how each plant is used. Another attraction is the wonderfully aromatic garden for the blind, which has explanation boards in Braille. There are also large sculptures, mostly made of wood, dotted throughout the gardens. The **tea garden** is very popular with locals and foreigners alike, and is run by volunteers from a number of local charitable organisations for fundraising purposes. Not to be missed are the crumpets, dripping with syrup and cream, and the scones – and the prices are probably the most reasonable in Durban. On certain Sundays throughout the year, when the KwaZulu-Natal Philharmonic Orchestra performs at the lake in the gardens, Durbanites flock there with their families, rugs and picnic baskets to enjoy the splendid music. Although entrance to the gardens is free, a fee is charged for these events.

OPPOSITE TOP *The colourful and noisy fishmongers in the Victoria Street Fish Market sell a variety of fresh fish caught along the KwaZulu-Natal coastline.*

OPPOSITE CENTRE *Beautiful red, yellow and burnt orange piles of spices displayed in brightly coloured plastic basins fill the Victoria Street Market with the thick smells of spicy curries and other exotic foods.*

OPPOSITE BOTTOM *Swirls of vibrantly coloured cloths can be found in the exotic sari shops in the Indian section of the city.*

ABOVE *Against the backdrop of the imposing Jumma Musjid Mosque, street traders display and sell bulbs, plants, roots and potions used by traditional healers.*

RIGHT *The cool and pretty Botanical Gardens are famous for their amazing collection of orchids as well as their indigenous medicinal plant display and garden for the blind.*

Greyville Racecourse

The large oval of Greyville Racecourse marks a great patch of green separating the city centre from the gentle slopes of Durban's residential Berea. It is here that the famous **July Handicap** is held every winter, drawing thousands of visitors, as much for the avant-garde fashions as for the racing horses. In the centre of the racecourse is the **Royal Durban Golf Course**, through the centre of which runs the canna-lined D.L.I. (Durban Light Infantry) Avenue, which leads to the suburb of Berea.

The Campbell Collections

High on the Berea, overlooking Durban, is a graceful old Cape Dutch-inspired home built for the wealthy sugar baron Marshall Campbell and his family. Today, Muckleneuk, as the house is called, is home to rare and unique archival resources that are renowned internationally as the Killie Campbell Africana Collections. It is also known as a venue for postgraduate research, and is a museum well worth visiting.

The **Killie Campbell Africana Library** has the world's best book collection on South Africa, together with a rich oral and photographic archive of the country's history covering the last two centuries. The **William Campbell Picture Collection** features some of the country's finest anthologies of work by black South African artists, such as Jabulani Ntuli, S.M.T. Mnguni and Gerard Benghu. Two hundred and fifty paintings of African tribal life and Zulu society and customs by Barbara Tyrell add vitality to the collection. The highlight, though, is definitely the **Mashu Museum of Ethnology** which contains the region's finest assemblages of African cultural artefacts. Utensils, weapons, carvings, masks, pottery and musical instruments are displayed alongside one of the finest collections of beadwork in the country. However, the collections can only be viewed by appointment.

Mitchell Park and Jameson Park

Situated in the leafy residential area of Berea, these two adjoining parks are a favourite place for Durban families. Children enjoy running around on the spacious lawns under the trees, there is a year-round, colourful floral display in the beds edging the gardens, as well as a beautiful rose garden, which is a real treat, and not just for rose enthusiasts. One section of the park that has been set aside as a **small zoo** features huge tortoises, a number of small animals and reptiles, tropical fish, and exotic birds in large aviaries.

The park's Blue Zoo Café serves a good breakfast and tea, has facilities for disabled people and a playground to keep the children entertained.

ABOVE *Dressing up forms part of the attraction at the annual Rothman's July Handicap at Greyville Racecourse.*

KwaZulu-Natal Society of Arts and the Durban Centre for Photography

Set in a leafy green park in the residential area of Glenwood is the small but sophisticated KwaZulu-Natal Society of Arts (KNSA). This beautifully designed gallery was specially commissioned to replace the old Natal Society of Arts, which was founded in 1905. It does not carry a permanent collection, but rather hosts regular exhibitions of work by established student and community artists, as well as the occasional exhibition of international work. A workshop caters for resident artists.

The Durban Centre for Photography (DCP) is based in the same building. In addition to the educational role played by the KNSA, the DCP also holds workshops and hosts local and international exhibitions of contemporary, historical, documentary, commercial and art photography.

The two-level **gallery shop** is crammed with a variety of artworks and collectibles, many beautifully made by local artists and crafters. Handmade paper, cards, candles, jewellery, cutlery, ceramics, glassware and woven cloth, much of it with an African theme, are on sale. But one of the nicest things about this venue is the **restaurant,** favoured by Durban's trendier set. A great selection of healthy foods and cakes is served either in- or outdoors under the umbrellas and trees.

Dalton Road Traditional Market

As you drive south along Sydney Road towards Umbilo, it is easy to miss the entrance to the Dalton Road Traditional Market. No signs mark its existence, neither from Sydney Road nor from Dalton Road, except for the drums and skins drying outside on the pavement. From the outside, it looks a bit daunting, placed as it is in an industrial area behind a busy bus stop. This 'market' is attached to the Dalton Road Hostel, which used to be a single-sex hostel for migrant labourers during the apartheid years.

Comprising a row of little cubicles along a passage, the market is where many urban Zulu people are able to buy their costumes and accessories needed for traditional ceremonies. Dalton Road is one of the main suppliers of traditional Zulu drums, shields, cowhide skirts, cow-tail switches and the elaborate head-dresses to Zulu people, and not necessarily to the tourist trade. This means that you are likely to be able to purchase authentic crafts and 'curios' for a lower price than anywhere else – other than in the rural areas.

However, it is advisable to visit the market with a Zulu-speaking guide, since many of the craftspeople are from rural backgrounds; although they may have lived in Durban for some time, they retain many of their traditions and customs, and few have mastered much English.

Kingspark Stadium

Almost all of Durban's sporting venues lie within an 8 kilometre radius of the city centre, with Kingspark Stadium being in the centre. The 60 000-seater stadium is used as a venue for rugby, soccer, athletics, cycling and even show-jumping. This is also the home of the Natal Sharks, KwaZulu-Natal's rugby team, and where the provincial heroes take to the field in their distinctive black and white gear to the frenzied delight of their fans. The Shark Tank – a shop at the stadium touted as an exciting shopping 'maul' – sells all kinds of rugby paraphernalia, the branded Natal Sharks merchandise being popular among rugby enthusiasts.

Kingspark also hosts top local soccer teams such as AmaZulu and African Wanderers, and until the 35 new sporting venues planned for the disadvantaged communities living in townships around the city are complete, this stadium will continue to host most of the major sports events. This is also the finishing/starting point of the Comrades Marathon (see page 50).

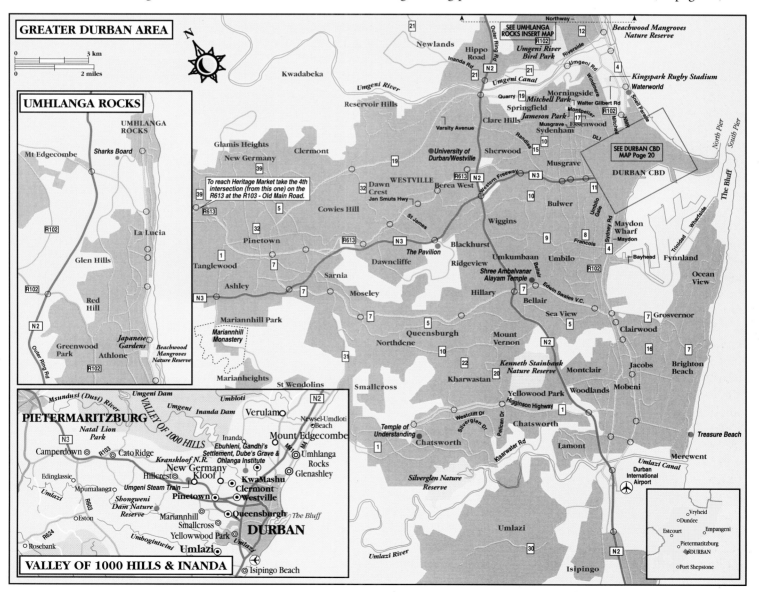

Durban – Bay City

NORTHERN DURBAN

As you head north out of Durban, you will cross the large Umgeni River, which has its source in the KwaZulu-Natal Midlands, towards the Drakensberg. On a good day, pelicans and numerous other water birds can be seen in the reeds. (The mouth of the Umgeni River is where the Dusi Canoe Marathon ends – *see* page 52.) Further north are the affluent suburbs of Durban North and Umhlanga Rocks, and the areas which, during the apartheid years, were designated 'black' areas, such as the sprawling townships of KwaMashu and Ntazuma and the 'Indian' areas of Phoenix, Inanda and Verulam. Some of the places of interest in these areas are difficult to find, so it is advisable to go with a local tour guide.

Umgeni River Bird Park

Take the M4 highway from Durban city centre, and as you cross the Umgeni River, turn off along Riverside Road to the Umgeni River Bird Park. Even if you are not a fan of captive birds, this bird park is impressive. Large **walk-through**

aviaries have elevated wooden walkways so that you can watch small birds in the tree canopy, walk through open paddocks and past cool waterfalls and lush tropical vegetation. The enclosures are clean, airy and well-kept, and the birds noisy and colourful. A 'baby room' with a viewing window allows visitors to see how chicks are reared by 'foster parents'.

One of the highlights of a visit to this world-class bird park is the highly educational (and entertaining) **free-flight bird show,** which is unique in Africa. Mischievous gaudy macaws whirl overhead, the huge, stately ground hornbill struts around the ring, and a Cape vulture and an African fish eagle put on a display, as do owls, storks and tiny parakeets. As these birds show off their beauty in free, unrestricted flight, their trainers give a commentary on the problems facing many species of bird which are on the critically endangered list, such as the wattled and blue cranes – also featured in the show.

In the centre of the park is an **open-air café** where you can spend an enjoyable time relaxing while watching both the birds and the passers-by.

OPPOSITE *A highlight at the Umgeni River Bird Park is the free-flight shows where birds are let out of their cages to fly free and entertain visitors, who delight in watching the magnificent African fish eagles with their haunting call of the wilderness* (TOP), *as well as the gaudy and raucous macaws which are put through their paces during the show* (CENTRE). *A number of other birds can also be seen at the park, such as the little red-billed teals, cautiously making their way through the watery reeds* (BOTTOM).

ABOVE *Bridges arch across the mouth and estuary of the Umgeni River, connecting the northern suburbs and the city centre.*

Beachwood Mangroves Nature Reserve

On the northern bank of the Umgeni River is one of the last vestiges of mangroves, a fascinating plant which was once prolific along the estuaries of KwaZulu-Natal's rivers. This unique ecosystem is the largest population of mangrove trees left in the Durban area, and they are protected by the surrounding Beachwood Mangroves Nature Reserve. The KwaZulu-Natal Nature Conservation Service has erected a wooden education centre and developed three **trails** around the reserve, where visitors can walk through the swamps and see the waders feeding on fiddler crabs and mudskippers, which are commonly associated with mangrove swamps.

Japanese Gardens

While still beautiful and green, Durban's Japanese Gardens have more of an air of oriental delicacy than of tropical lushness often associated with gardens on South Africa's eastern seaboard. Small stone pagodas and tinkly waterfalls complement the grassy lawns. Little red-painted bridges curve

neatly over lily-filled ponds which attract a variety of water birds. The gardens, with their unusual beauty, attract not just the usual families on their weekend picnics – although there are many of them too – but also wedding parties. On weekends, it is a delight to sit on the lawns and watch elaborately dressed brides with their colourful entourages of bridesmaids and families having their photographs taken under the trees.

Umhlanga Rocks

Many people prefer the beaches of Umhlanga Rocks to those of Durban, but during the peak season they are much the same: busy and very crowded. High-rise buildings, hotels and holiday apartments line the coast as far as the Ohlanga River, but one of the last remaining areas of dune forest in prime condition can be found on the Ohlanga River Lagoon.

This area is encompassed by a lovely nature reserve through which runs the small but delightful **Umhlanga Nature Trail**. Along the trail, which wanders through the dunes, swamp areas and forest for about an hour and a half, a number of birds may

be spotted, as well as the comical vervet monkey, some duiker and shy bushbuck. Across the lagoon towards the north, it is possible to see the remnants of an **Early Iron Age midden,** dating back as far as AD 600. The midden was exposed and subsequently discovered when the river flooded.

If you visit the nature reserve and happen to stumble upon pottery shards, do not to remove any.

OPPOSITE TOP *A Hindu bride and groom celebrate their wedding with heavy garlands of brightly coloured flowers. Over weekends, colourful wedding parties can often be seen having their photographs taken at the Japanese Gardens.*

OPPOSITE BOTTOM *Small painted bridges, wooden pagodas covered in trailing plants and great tree ferns decorate the lawns of the Japanese Gardens.*

ABOVE *Against the backdrop of hotels and distant sugar-cane fields, the Umhlanga Rocks lighthouse stands sentinel over the beach, guiding ships along the coast.*

At the southern end of Umhlanga Rocks town, directly in front of the old and elegant Oyster Box Hotel with its lawns running down onto the beach, is Umhlanga's pretty red and white **lighthouse.**

Sharks Board

Situated in Umhlanga Rocks, the Sharks Board is one of the world's foremost shark research institutes. Apart from doing research, the Sharks Board maintains the offshore nets along the province's swimming beaches, and every morning boats go out to check the nets. If any sharks have been caught in the nets and died, they are brought back to the institute.

It is possible to visit the Sharks Board headquarters, an outing that is both informative and fascinating. Inside are display cases and massive fibreglass models of sharks and dolphins leaping through the air. The walls are pasted with old newspaper cuttings about the many shark attacks that used to occur in the past before the nets were used. An impressive audio-visual show outlines the work of the board. You then go outside to the little amphitheatre where a shark is dissected – and horror stories are told of what can sometimes be found in the stomach contents.

Gandhi Settlement

Many foreign visitors do not know that Mahatma Gandhi spent 21 years in South Africa, before returning to his native India. He arrived in the country in 1893 and in 1903 established a settlement of about 100 acres in what was then rural Phoenix, about 25 kilometres north of central Durban in an area which today edges on the enormous township of Inanda. The Zulu people of this area named the bordering informal settlement *Bhambayi* (their version of the word 'Bombay' in reference to the Indian settlement). The inhabitants of Gandhi's *ashram* farmed and led a life of self-sufficiency in accordance with his philosophy of *Sarvodaya*, or 'the ideal life'. It was on this farm that Gandhi began to formulate his ideas and organise the Indian passive resistance campaign against the racist laws of the apartheid government. It was also here that he established his newspaper, the *Indian Opinion*. The façade of the building which housed the newspaper press still stands.

Sadly, not much remains of his settlement which was violently destroyed by squatters from the surrounding Inanda township in 1985, when the Indians were forced to flee for their lives. Many of the remaining ruins are presently inhabited by squatters. However, if all goes according to an ambitious and costly plan, the settlement will be restored and a museum of sorts established. Negotiations are underway to resettle the squatters elsewhere. In the meanwhile, even though there is not much to see, it is thrilling to be able to stand on the floor of a room where the great spiritual and political leader once slept.

The Gandhi settlement is quite difficult to locate in the rambling shacklands of Inanda, so it is advisable to join one of several guided township tours.

Ohlanga Institute and Rev John Dube's Grave

Large, straggly eucalyptus trees stand sentinel over the graves of Reverend John Langalibalele Dube and his wife, which are on a shady hill overlooking the sprawling townships near Durban city centre and the sea. As with the Gandhi settlement, it is advisable to join a guided tour. Remember that you need to observe the courtesy and custom of first stopping at the Dube family house to ask permission to visit the gravesite.

Reverend Dube, the first president of the African National Congress (ANC), was a writer, clergyman, teacher, political leader and great humanitarian. He was born in 1871 and was buried on the scenic hillside overlooking Durban in 1946, having donated his land to the education trust he had founded. The trust was originally known as the Zulu Christian Industrial School, which later became famous as the Ohlanga Institute, a focal point for the education of young Africans. The original school curriculum was based on similar principles as the nearby Gandhi settlement, which is only one kilometre away and can be seen clearly from the gravesite. Generations of children were taught and encouraged at the Ohlanga Institute to become self-sufficient during a time when quality education for black students was almost unheard of.

Ebuhleni

One of the most fascinating and colourful sects in Durban's spiritual life is the 400 000-member Shembe church (or Ibandla Iama Nazaretha). Followers of the prophet Shembe combine a blend of Christian and traditional beliefs, with dance being the primary form of worship.

The prophet Shembe was born in 1870 and died in 1935. With the spread of Christianity, he was inspired to form what was one of the first independent churches in southern Africa, originally known as the *AmaNazaretha* church.

During the dark years of apartheid, the Shembe citadel, Ebuhleni, sheltered the landless and dispossessed, and has since become well known as a centre for black self-advancement, pursuing a strong craft-based work ethic.

Two important **Shembe festivals** are held every year, and are well worth attending. The first, held in January, is the occasion when followers make a pilgrimage to the 'Holy Mountain' on the first Sunday of every new year, retracing the route taken by the prophet Shembe. It is led by clergy and traditional chiefs (*amakhosi*) and sets out from Ebuhleni, Shembe's citadel, overlooking the Inanda Dam. They march 60 kilometres north to Ndwedwe, reaching the Holy Mountain late on the second day. Each pilgrim ascends the mountain and places a stone on the great *isivivane*, a huge cairn alongside which a service is held. The ceremonies are colourful and energetic with much singing taking place.

The second festival is a month-long festival that takes place in July. Visitors are welcome and have ample opportunity to view the spectacular ceremonies where the faithful of the Holy Church of Nazareth Baptists – shield-waving warriors, young men in kilts and pith helmets, bare-breasted maidens and traditional matrons – don their best and dance in worship of God. The perfectly choreographed, if somewhat frenzied and up-tempo dancing, is usually accompanied by *imbomu* – long, deep-toned horns, whose vibrations sink deep into the bones, and pulsing drums. It is believed that the prophet Shembe saw the uniforms worn by the followers in a dream, and some wonderful cross-cultural costumes may be seen.

If you find that you are unable to attend either of the two main festivals, ask one of the township tour operators to take you to any of the regular Shembe ceremonies or Sunday services. The Shembe are used to visitors, who are always welcome. The evocative singing will certainly move you, and you may be lucky enough to witness a baptism – where members of the church are often healed during rituals steeped in symbolism.

OPPOSITE TOP AND BOTTOM *The imposing golden steeples of the Hare Krishna Temple of Understanding in Chatsworth are a unique architectural feature in South Africa* (TOP). *Also noteworthy are the enormous murals depicting the life and times of Lord Krishna* (BOTTOM).

WESTERN DURBAN

As with northern and southern Durban, the suburbs to the west of the city centre and away from the sea were divided into distinctly 'Black', 'Asian or Indian' and 'White' areas during the apartheid years. Closer to the city are what used to be the more affluent white suburbs of Westville, Hillcrest and Kloof. It is here that you will find the big shopping malls such as The Pavilion, and also the fairly twee, but pretty, Heritage Market. Other highlights west of central Durban, apart from the many small nature reserves, include the Temple of Understanding in Chatsworth, the Mariannhill Monastery, and, of course, the breathtaking Valley of a Thousand Hills, which is best seen from the Rob Roy Hotel in the residential area of Botha's Hill.

Temple of Understanding

One of the easiest way to get to the Hare Krishna Temple of Understanding is to catch a bus from Warwick Street Triangle in the city centre. But if that seems too much for you, you can join a guided tour that will take you through the hustle and bustle of the surrounding suburb of Chatsworth. The busy residential area and the slightly jaded look of the exterior of the temple belies the sense of peace and tranquillity and the opulence to be found inside. The amazing golden steeples are unique in this country and were designed and built by the International Society for Krishna Consciousness. The inside of the domed roof is adorned with massive depictions of the life and times of Lord Krishna, and the smell of incense gently pervades the air. Be prepared to leave your shoes at the entrance when entering the temple. When planning your visit, keep in mind that the temple **restaurant** is renowned for its vegetarian food served at lunch time.

Silverglen Nature Reserve and Nursery

It is estimated that 80 per cent of southern Africa's population consults traditional healers. Traditional healers, in their turn, use a wide variety of indigenous plants to treat their patients. More than 400 species of plant are used by healers in KwaZulu-Natal alone, and over 1 500 tonnes of plant are traded annually in the province. The growing population together with the increased use of traditional medicine is putting tremendous pressure on indigenous medicinal plants.

But on the outskirts of Durban, in the residential suburb of Chatsworth, lies the Silverglen Nature Reserve and, within it, the famous Silverglen Nursery – known as one of the first nurseries in the country to work towards finding a solution to the drop in numbers of the more frequently used indigenous medicinal plants. The nursery runs training courses for traditional healers, which include the propagation and growing of medicinal plants. Extensive courses are also run for anyone who is interested in indigenous gardening. The nursery also supplies and sells many of its indigenous seedlings and plants to the public.

Marriannhill Monastery

For hundreds of years, Christian missionaries played a significant and influential role in South African history. The Trappist monks were particularly active in KwaZulu-Natal and founded the magnificent Mariannhill Monastery in 1882, building it over a number of years in hilly surroundings just outside Durban. From here, many other smaller missions sprang up throughout the province. Self-reliance was one of the main tenets of the Trappists who, when constructing the monastery, used materials – including the stained glass windows – made by the craftsmen-monks themselves, and the glorious building is testimony to their restraint and discipline.

Today the monastery complex is still fairly self-sufficient. It encompasses surrounding farmlands, a large herb and vegetable garden, a bakery, a factory where candles are made by hand, schools and accommodation units. The small chapel is famous for its beautifully crafted wooden interior. Within the complex is the more elaborate **St Joseph's Cathedral,** which itself is a work of art because of its wall-painting, sculpture and architectural form. In order to appreciate the beauty of St Joseph's, attend a Sunday service, which will give you a more holistic and realistic appreciation of the monastery life-style and values.

A number of beautiful books and pamphlets are available, giving information about the role of the monastery, and further information can be obtained at the little **monastery shop.** Here you can also buy candles and other monastic bric-a-brac and, depending on the day of the week, fresh, warm bread.

The Pavilion

As you approach Durban on the N3 from Pietermaritzburg, the large glass domes and flags of Durban's busiest shopping mall, The Pavilion, looms on the horizon. An elegant, up-market mall, it draws approximately one million shoppers a month and, during the busy season, cars often have to park on the freeway approach. The two-storey mall houses huge supermarket chains, sports and fashion shops, speciality retail outlets and a large movie house. All the usual international fast-food outlets can be found alongside coffee shops, book shops and baby shops. In the centre aisles of the mall are wagon vendors selling crafts and bits and bobs.

Shongweni Resource Reserve

Venture about 25 minutes out of Durban on the N3 towards Pietermaritzburg and you feel as if you are in the middle of the African bush. Shongweni Resource Reserve is conveniently situated between two of the province's busiest urban centres and yet still retains a sense of the wildness of Africa. A wide variety of game can be seen, including buffalo, giraffe, warthog, zebra, waterbuck, the elusive black-backed jackal, wildebeest and kudu, and more than 200 species of bird have been recorded in this little reserve.

A small but delightful eight-bedded **bushcamp** nestles against the slopes of Mkongoma Hill, from which the camp takes its name. Here you can sip sundowners on the veranda and watch

---

TOP *Colourful flags billow above The Pavilion, Durban's busiest shopping mall.*

OPPOSITE TOP *Two young Zulu boys in the Valley of a Thousand Hills, a rural area some 30 minutes' drive from the city centre.*

OPPOSITE BOTTOM *The Shree Ambalvanar Alayam Second River Temple with its brightly painted depictions of Hindu Gods is one of many Hindu temples in the city, and has been declared a national monument.*

Umgeni Steam Train

In 1982, a group of steam train enthusiasts formed the Umgeni Steam Railway. Realising that the demise of steam rail in South Africa was not too far off, the group restored and re-established one of the oldest lines along one of the country's most scenic railway routes. On the last Sunday of every month, the delightful steam train chugs away from the old Kloof Station in Kloof which has been turned into a **railside pub and restaurant.** The train is sometimes hired out for functions and conferences, with all the proceeds channelled back into restoration.

game come down to the river to drink. The camp is self-catering, but there is a game guard on hand to assist you, and even more appealing, a camp cook who will prepare your meals while you sit back and enjoy the stunning view. **Game drives** can be arranged, and there are also horse and **hiking trails.**

Heritage Market

Hillcrest is one of Durban's leafy upmarket suburbs, and at the entrance to the village is the quaint, rather twee, Heritage Market. There is a certain olde-world charm to the 'Victorian' village with its 160 speciality shops selling anything from home-made cheese, fresh fish, new-age paraphernalia, clothing, collectors' books and antiques. Some open-air cafés, tea gardens and restaurants are located in the village, and on weekends there are often performances by classical or jazz musicians and choirs in the small, Victorian bandstand, which is surrounded by a rose-filled garden.

Valley of a Thousand Hills and Valley Trust

About 45 kilometres northwest of Durban (N3), a short distance past the village of Hillcrest, you will find yourself in rural KwaZulu-Natal. Stop off at the **Rob Roy Hotel** for tea on the front lawn and from here you will see stretching before you the Valley of a Thousand Hills – the name aptly describing the plunging gorges and bush-covered hills. It is a magnificent view, misty and mysterious during the rainy summer months, and crisp and cold during winter. The road up the hill is the old route to Pietermaritzburg, dotted with farmstalls, craft shops, tea-rooms and a number of small restaurants.

The inhabitants of the valley are generally poor and disadvantaged, and it was because of this that **Valley Trust** was established as a small clinic to assist these people. From small beginnings, Valley Trust has grown into a large organisation providing numerous services not only to the people from the valley, but also to other communities in the area. The Trust provides training in organic gardening, primary health care, pre- and post-natal care, building and poultry care, and a number of other useful tools for self-reliance or for becoming a small entrepreneur. A tour of the premises is highly educational, and **backpacker accommodation** is also provided.

SOUTH-CENTRAL

The southern section of Durban has fewer tourist attractions than other parts of the city, but there are a number of places of interest worth visiting. Parts of the southern suburbs are the city's oldest and were once inhabited by Durban's Indian population. The long ridge which juts out into the sea, known as 'the Bluff', protects Durban's harbour.

Shree Ambalvanar Alayam Second River Temple

A number of small, beautiful and elaborately painted Hindu temples, many very old, are found in Durban. Many of the important Hindu festivals, such as *Kavadi* and *Ratha Yatra*, where devotees practise fire-walking, walk on nail beds and undergo body-piercing, are centred around these temples and shrines. One of the most spectacular and well known is the Shree Ambalvanar Alayam Second River Temple in Bellair Road, Cato Manor, which has been declared a national monument. The exterior of the shrine is decorated with brightly painted depictions of Hindu gods such as Vishnu, Shiva and Ganesha. The magnificent doors were salvaged from a temple which was built on the banks of the Umbilo River in 1875 and which was subsequently destroyed by floods.

The Bluff and Treasure Beach

Legend has it that the Zulu name for Durban – *eThekweni* – is taken from the shape of the bay formed by the Bluff, which the Zulu people said resembled the hanging testicles of a bull. The Bluff today is largely residential, although there are plans afoot to develop an old army base at the sea-end of the Bluff for tourism. Its inside edge flanks the harbour in the north, but further south are a number of industries, including oil refineries and Durban's airport. Along the outside edge are several popular beaches, which are not as crowded as the city beaches, and **Cave Rock**, a world-renowned surfing spot, known for its big and dangerous waves. At the far southern section of the Bluff lies Treasure Beach, where the Wildlife and Environment Society of Southern Africa (WESSA) has established a nature reserve and environmental education centre. Many students have spent time at Treasure Beach learning about the marine and coastal ecosystems. WESSA also conducts **guided night-time beach walks** for visitors.

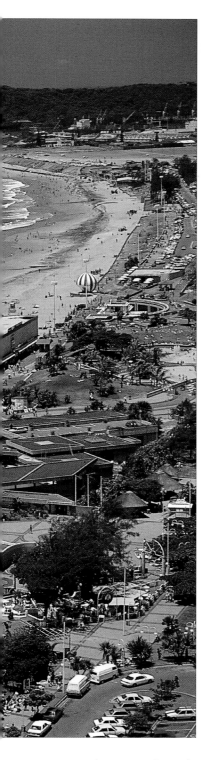

ABOVE *Looking southwards onto Durban's famous beachfront area, Seaworld and the Dolphinarium, South Beach, Addington Beach and Vetch's Pier edge the coastline as it curves into the harbour. In the background, the Bluff protects the southern entrance to the bay.*

USEFUL INFORMATION

The tourism information office at Tourist Junction houses the offices of KwaZulu Tourism, Durban Africa and KwaZulu-Natal Conservation Services. A number of tour operators can also be found here.

African Art Centre: Tourist Junction, 160 Pine Street, Durban, tel. (031) 304-7915

Bartle Arts Trust (BAT): Along the harbour quayside, off the Esplanade, tel. (031) 332-0468 or (031) 337-8451

Beachwood Mangroves Nature Reserve: off Riverside Road, Durban North, tel. (031) 83-5591

Botanical Gardens: cnr Botanic Gardens and Sydenham roads, Musgrave, Durban, tel. (031) 201-1303

Campbell Collections: 22 Marriot Road, Berea, Durban, tel. (031) 207-3432

City Hall and Post Office: West Street, Durban, tel. (031) 300-6911

Cultural History Museum: cnr Aliwal and Smith streets, Durban, tel. (031) 300-6241

Dalton Road Traditional Market: Dalton Road, Umbilo, Durban, (no telephone)

Durban Cultural and Documentation Centre: cnr Epsom Road and Derby Street, Greyville, Durban, tel. (031) 309-7559

Ebuhleni (Shembe Church): Contact Tourist Junction (*see* below)

Fitzsimons Snake Park: 24a Lower Marine Parade, Durban, tel. (031) 337-6456

Gandhi Settlement: contact Tourist Junction (*see* below)

Hambe Kahle Tours: Tourist Junction, 160 Pine Street, Durban, tel. (031) 305-5586

Heritage Market: 9 Old Main Road, Hillcrest, tel. (031) 765-2500

International Conference Centre (ICC): Walnut Road, Durban, tel. (031) 360-1000

Japanese Gardens: Tinsley Road, Durban North, tel. (031) 83-1333

Jumma Musjid Mosque: cnr Grey and Queen streets, Durban, tel. (031) 307-4786

Kingspark Stadium: Walter Gilbert Road, Durban, tel. (031) 23-6368

KwaMuhle Museum: 130 Ordinance Road, Durban, tel. (031) 300-3610

KwaZulu-Natal Society of Arts and Durban

Centre for Photography: 166 Bulwer Road, Glenwood, Durban, tel. (031) 202-2293

Mariannhill Monastery: 1 Abbot Francis Road, Mariannhill, tel. (031) 700-4288

Natural History Museum: Durban City Hall, Smith Street, Durban, tel. (031) 309-7559

Ohlanga Institute: contact Tourist Junction (*see* below), or Langa Dube in Inanda, tel. (031) 510-1555

Pavilion, the: 8 Spine Road, Westville, Durban, tel. (031) 265-0558, fax (031) 265-0367

Playhouse Company, the: 231 Smith Street, Durban, tel. (031) 369-9555

Port Natal Maritime Museum: Maritime Place, Victoria Embankment, Durban, tel. (031) 300-6323

Rob Roy Hotel: Rob Roy Crescent, Botha's Hill, tel. (031) 777-1305

Seaworld, Dolphinarium and Oceanographic Research Institute: Marine Parade, Durban, tel. (031) 337-3536

Sharks Board: cnr Umhlanga Rocks and Hickary drives, Umhlanga Rocks, tel. (031) 566-1001

Shongweni Resource Reserve: Private Bag 1020, Hillcrest, 3650, tel. (031) 769-1283

Shree Ambalvanar Alayam Second River Temple: 890 Bellair Road, Cato Manor, Durban, tel. (031) 261-8114

Silverglen Nursery: Lakeview Drive, Chatsworth, Durban, tel. (013) 404-5628

Temple of Understanding: Bhaktieedanta Sami Road, Chatsworth, Durban, tel. (031) 430-3367

Tourist Junction: First Floor, Old Station Building, 160 Pine Street, Durban, tel. (031) 304-4934, fax (031) 304-6196, e-mail: funinsun@iafrica.com

Umgeni River Bird Park: 490 Riverside Road, Durban North, tel. (031) 579-4600

Umgeni Steam Train: Kloof Station, Kloof, Durban, tel. (031) 86-6191

Valley Trust: Zulu Reserve Road, Botha's Hill, tel. (031) 777-1955

Waterworld: Marine Parade, Durban, tel. (031) 337-6336

Wildlife and Environment Society of Southern Africa (Treasure Beach): 835 Marine Drive, The Bluff, Durban, tel. (031) 467-8507

Workshop, the: cnr Aliwal and Commercial streets, Durban, tel. (031) 304-9894

Pietermaritzburg –
The Last Outpost

LEFT *Pietermaritzburg's handsome Victorian City Hall, reputedly the biggest red-brick building in the southern hemisphere, is a famous landmark in the city (see page 48).*

ABOVE *Another testimony to the city's colonial past is Queen Victoria's statue, which stands outside the Parliament Building in Longmarket Street.*

PIETERMARITZBURG – THE LAST OUTPOST

Publicity House • City Hall • Tatham Art Gallery • Natal Museum • Voortrekker Museum • Statue of Gandhi
Alexandra Park • Macrorie House Museum • Natal National Botanical Gardens • World's View

Eighty kilometres northwest of Durban along the N3 lies a city which used to be known as the 'last British outpost', in reference to its colonial past and its beautiful Victorian red-brick architecture. Pietermaritzburg takes its name from Voortrekker leaders Piet Retief, who was murdered by the Zulu King Dingane, and Gerrit Maritz. In 1838, the Voortrekkers, having trekked from the Cape in their wagons, laid the foundations of Pietermaritzburg hoping to make it their new capital. However, they clashed fiercely with the Zulu people before the British finally took over and made Pietermaritzburg a military garrison in 1843. The city has many landmarks dating back to that time, and it is possible to take a self-guided **Town Trail,** passing no less than 50 national monuments as you wander around the city.

Pietermaritzburg has always been considered a bit of a sleepy hollow, but it is, along with Ulundi in Zululand, the co-capital of KwaZulu-Natal, boasting a university and a number of the country's top schools. In spring, the massive jacaranda trees which line many streets break into soft mauve blossoms; in summer the temperatures can be scorching – although, without the coastal humidity – and winters are cold and crisp.

Publicity House

This classic red-brick building, erected in 1884 to house the then colonial Borough Police, is today the home of Pietermaritzburg's Publicity Association. In this lovely old building visitors can obtain information, join tours and collect pamphlets with details about the city and surrounding areas.

It is interesting to note that it was the bell tower in this building, which, during the apartheid years, was used to ring the nine o'clock curfew signalling all black South Africans to be off the city streets.

City Hall

Not only is Pietermaritzburg's City Hall a magnificent example of classical Victorian architecture, but the red-brick structure is reputedly the largest all-brick structure in the southern hemisphere. Built in 1900, it stands on the corner of Church and Commercial streets, and its pretty clock tower keeps city workers on time. Other notable features are its ornate gables, domes and stained-glass windows. Inside, large wooden staircases sweep to the upper floors, and from the galleries, you can look down into the main hall with its old organ pipes.

ABOVE *As the leaves begin to change colour and flutter to the ground in the Natal National Botanical Gardens, a Scottish band plays a haunting tune. The gardens are located about 4 kilometres from the city centre, off Mayor's Walk (see page 52).*

OPPOSITE LEFT *Publicity House, in Commercial Street.*

OPPOSITE RIGHT *This elegant Victorian building which houses the Tatham Art Gallery was once home to the Old Supreme Court.*

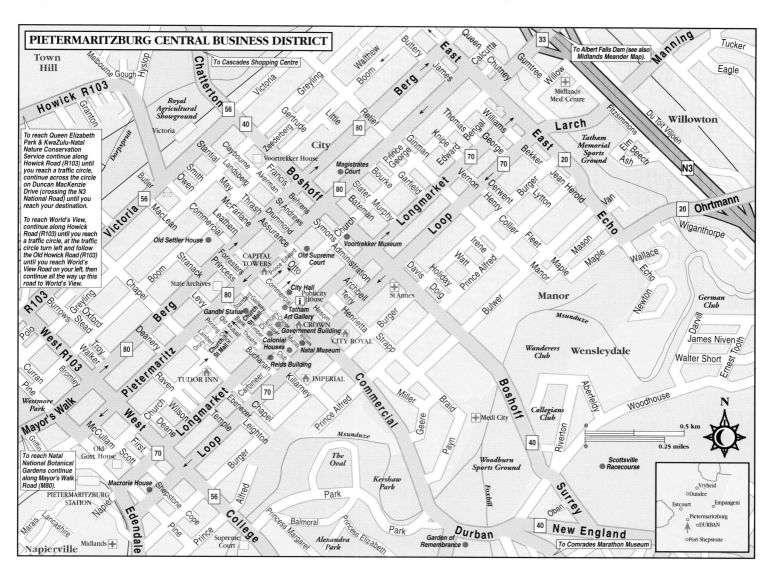

Tatham Art Gallery

Directly across the road from Publicity House and the City Hall is the Tatham Art Gallery, housed in the Old Supreme Court building, and yet another of Pietermaritzburg's gracious old red-brick Victorian buildings. The gallery has excellent permanent collections of works by black and white South African artists, as well as displays of beadwork, basketry and other traditional crafts. A display of particular interest is that of the ear-lobe plugs which were once part of traditional Zulu attire. These days, earplugs of this nature are seldom seen, except occasionally in the deep rural areas of the province such as Msinga. The museum has a vibrant and active education division which holds a variety of short courses, talks and workshops. It also has a full calendar of visiting exhibitions.

Upstairs, with a balcony overlooking the small gardens, the busy streets of Pietermaritzburg and the City Hall, is a small **restaurant and coffee shop** that serves an excellent light lunch and a variety of tea-time cakes – and where even the chairs are works of art. In the adjacent old Presbyterian Church, the **Phemba Kahle Project** stages drama and music, as well as craft bazaars and classes.

Natal Museum

Centrally situated along Loop Street, the Natal Museum lies within a short walking distance of the City Hall and the Tatham Art Gallery. It is a delightful contrast of modern display techniques and relics from the past, reflecting a museum in transition. One of South Africa's five national museums, it is home to several of the country's greatest national collections, such as one of the most extensive shell collections in the southern hemisphere.

The natural science hall on the ground floor of the museum features massive displays of dinosaurs, including the giant *Tyrannosaurus rex*, old painted dioramas, some interesting but rather moth-eaten African mammals, and birds that are indigenous to KwaZulu-Natal. A glimpse of life beneath the ocean can be seen on the 'undersea' walk. But perhaps some of the most interesting displays are those depicting South Africa's human history. There is a recreation of a Drakensberg cave with original San (Bushmen) paintings, a wreck of a Portuguese trading vessel used during the sixteenth century, Zulu artefacts, and an up-to-date collection of apartheid-era items such as old street signs, T-shirts, posters, flags, photographs, and musical and domestic instruments. A 'Victorian lane' gives insight into settler life in Pietermaritzburg during the latter half of the nineteenth century.

Voortrekker Museum

From Publicity House, go down Longmarket Street, or head down Church Street from the City Hall, to reach the Voortrekker Museum. It is a small museum, but one of immense importance to many Afrikaans-speaking South

Comrades Marathon and Museum

It may have the reputation of being a sleepy hollow, but Pietermaritzburg is home to two internationally renowned sporting events: the Dusi Canoe Marathon (*see* page 52) and the gruelling Comrades Marathon, which takes place each year in June. The 88-kilometre-long race is run between Pietermaritzburg and Durban – alternating direction each year – and it attracts more the 13 000 long-distance runners from all over the world. The original race was the vision of an ex-World War I veteran, Victor Clapham, who wanted to remember those who had fallen in the war.

The first Comrades Marathon was run on 24 May 1921 with a mere 24 entrants, of whom only 16 made it to Durban. Little did anyone realise that so popular would the race become, with all its camaraderie, that more than 70 years later, it would still be run annually as one of the world's great ultra-distance marathons. Each year, on Comrades Marathon day, people rise early and flock to both the starting and the finishing points of the race. The excitement is palpable as the streets of the two cities and the freeways in between become clogged with spectators cooking their breakfasts or setting up their deckchairs on the roadside, waiting for the runners to pass.

The fascinating Comrades Marathon Museum is situated in a beautifully restored red-brick building called Comrades Marathon House, near the university.

Africans. It is situated in the original, restored **Church of the Vow,** a church that was built to commemorate one of the Boers' decisive battles against the Zulu.

Before the Battle of Blood River (*see* page 96), the Boer leader Andries Pretorius vowed that, should God grant the Boers victory over the Zulu, they would build this church. Approximately 3 000 Zulus died in that battle, while the Boers suffered no injuries. Today, the building, which was constructed in typical Cape-Dutch style in 1841, houses a variety of Voortrekker artefacts which include Piet Retief's prayer book, an old wagon and flintlock rifles. Next door to the museum is the small thatch-roofed cottage that once belonged to Andries Pretorius. It has also been restored and is open to the public.

picnics and late-afternoon strolls. A cycle track is used by cyclists to train for races, and under the cricket stand is a small, popular restaurant called **The Pavilion.** Tables are set out in and around the bandstand, and a pleasant afternoon can be whiled away sipping tea and watching a game of cricket.

On the first and last Sunday of each month, a large arts and crafts **flea market** is held under the trees, where a selection of handcrafted goods, clothes, leatherwork, woodwork and a number of other home-made goodies are sold. One of the annual premier events to take place in the park is the Gordon Verhoef and Krause **Art in the Park** exhibition. For five days in May each year, 60 or so of South Africa's top artists gather to display their work under the trees, and there is a tea garden, wine-tasting events and a number of musical performances. 'Art in the Park' is South Africa's largest outdoor art exhibition.

OPPOSITE TOP *A giant cockroach and ant climb the wall at the entrance to the Natal Museum, inside which a delightful array of displays awaits the visitor.*

OPPOSITE BOTTOM *Photographs and other memorabilia of old Boer families can be seen at the Voortrekker Museum in Long-market Street.*

LEFT *Mahatma Gandhi is remembered by South Africans for his admirable campaign of non-violent resistance against the apartheid government.*

BELOW *The white filigree ironwork of the Victorian bandstand and the red-brick buildings of the old pavilion at Alexandra Park are typical of the colonial architecture of the city.*

Statue of Gandhi

Part of Pietermaritzburg's Church Street has been transformed into a busy pedestrian shopping mall with shady trees under which vendors ply their trade. Only delivery vehicles are allowed to use the mall. In the centre of Church Street, in front of the Colonial Building, is a statue of Mahatma Gandhi. In 1893 Gandhi, who had come to South Africa as a lawyer, was thrown off a train at Pietermaritzburg Station because he was travelling in a 'whites-only' compartment. The statue was erected to mark the centenary of this event which is said to have been the start of Gandhi's campaign of non-violence.

Alexandra Park

The green lawns, winding paths, Victorian bandstand and cricket oval of Alexandra Park make it a favourite with Pietermaritzburg's residents. The Msundusi River meanders through the centre of the park and leafy green trees create the ideal setting for

Macrorie House Museum

Another fine example of the province's colonial past is the lovely old residence of Bishop Macrorie, who lived here from about 1870 to 1892. The house has a beautiful corrugated-iron roof and ornate ironwork typical of colonial Pietermaritzburg, and it has been furnished in period style. Macrorie House Museum is right at the end of Loop and Pine streets, and although many of the surrounding houses have undergone modern renovations, this one still imparts a sense of Pietermaritzburg's colonial past.

Natal National Botanical Gardens

These elegant 49-hectare gardens are a showcase for the indigenous flora of KwaZulu-Natal. They were established in 1874 and are situated on a hillside rolling down onto an ancient flood plain where the Dorpspruit River joins the Msundusi.

Dusi Canoe Marathon

The famous Dusi Canoe Marathon takes place annually between Pietermaritzburg and Durban, late in the rainy summer season. When the race first began back in the early 1960s, canoes were still made of wood and canvas, and there are exciting tales of breakages and river-side repairs. The marathon has become so popular over the years that numbers are now restricted to 20 000 canoeists.

Canoeists leave Pietermaritzburg in batches, paddling downstream for the entire length of the Msundusi River (fondly known to locals as the Dusi), negotiating rapids, weirs, paddling furiously across long stretches of still-water dams, and, in some cases, when the river is either too dangerous or too dry, they have to run, carrying their canoes with them.

The race organisers have taken the opportunity presented by the high profile of the race to raise awareness among South Africans about issues such as water pollution and wise water-use practices.

Shooting the rapids at the annual Dusi Canoe Marathon between Pietermaritzburg and Durban.

The original objective behind the cultivation of the gardens was to provide the early settlers with plants for their farms and plantations, but, over the years, they have developed into beautiful gardens featuring magnificent examples of southern hemisphere plants.

The gardens are divided into two sections – the **Indigenous Garden** and the **Exotic Garden** – with paths winding under massive trees, such as swamp cypresses, camphor and giant figs. Many of the southern hemisphere tree and plant species in the gardens are the last of their kind in the country.

Unlike the coastal regions of KwaZulu-Natal, where the climate does not change radically, Pietermaritzburg has marked seasonal changes, which means that the gardens, too, are constantly changing. Spring heralds an abundance of flowers; during summer the foliage is dense and lush; autumn brings wonderful orange and gold tones to the leaves; and during winter the stark, bare branches are almost sculptural.

More than 100 bird species have been recorded here, including the rare purple heron and four types of kingfisher,

and there are a number of small antelope, monkeys and mongooses. Occasionally an otter can also been spotted along the river bank.

A lovely **restaurant** serves breakfast, lunch and teas under the trees and umbrellas, or indoors, when the weather is bad. Close to the restaurant is a lily-filled duck pond where children can feed the water birds.

World's View

World's View is situated at the top of a plateau leading down into Pietermaritzburg, a route used in the nineteenth century by the Voortrekkers on their wagon trail from the Cape, and later by transport riders. The wagon trail road has been declared a national monument and forms part of Pietermaritzburg's **Green Belt Trails.** It is a lovely spot from which to orientate yourself and on a clear day to enjoy a spectacular view of the city and the surrounding countryside, including the Msundusi valley. In the warmer months, World's View is popular at full moon, and for champagne breakfasts and sundowners. A number of memorial plaques mark the site, and a display diagram shows the main features in the outlying landscape, as well as the route taken by the Voortrekkers.

OPPOSITE *The lily ponds and lush greenery draw numerous birds, including some rare species, to the Natal National Botanical Gardens on the outskirts of the city.*

ABOVE *Ramblers enjoy the many delights of hiking through the forests of Ferncliff, which are part of Pietermaritzburg's popular Green Belt Trails.*

USEFUL INFORMATION

The tourist information office is located in Publicity House in the city centre and provides information on both the city and the surrounding areas. The city is also home to the KwaZulu-Natal Conservation Service, which has its headquarters at Queen Elizabeth Park.

Alexandra Park Markets: Pietermaritzburg Tourism, Publicity House, 177 Commercial Road, Pietermaritzburg, tel. (033) 345-1348
City Hall: Commercial Road, Pietermaritzburg. For tours of the building, contact Pietermaritzburg Tourism (*see* below).
Comrades Marathon Museum: Connaught Road, Pietermaritzburg, tel. (033) 394-3512
Ecabazini Zulu Cultural Homestead: PO Box 13351, Cascades, Pietermaritzburg, 3202, tel. (033) 342-1928
KwaZulu-Natal Nature Conservation Service: Queen Elizabeth Park, PO Box 13069, Cascades, 3202, tel. (033) 845-1000, fax (033) 845-1001, e-mail: bookings@rhino.org.za
Macrorie House Museum: cnr Loop and Pine streets, Pietermaritzburg, tel. (033) 394-2161
Natal Museum: 237 Loop Street, Pietermaritzburg, tel. (033) 345-1404
Natal National Botanical Gardens: Off Mayor's Walk, Pietermaritzburg, tel. (033) 344-3585
Pietermaritzburg Tourism: Publicity House, 177 Commercial Road, Pietermaritzburg, tel. (033) 345-1348, fax (033) 394-3535, e-mail: ppa@futurenet.co.za
Tatham Art Gallery: Commercial Road, Pietermaritzburg, tel. (033) 342-1804
Voortrekker Museum: cnr Longmarket and Boshoff streets, Pietermaritzburg, tel. (033) 394-6834

The Midlands –
Creative Countryside

LEFT *Trout-fishing in the well-stocked dams and streams of the KwaZulu-Natal Midlands is a favourite pastime among locals and visitors alike (see box on page 59).*

ABOVE *Zulu women at Shuttleworth Weaving near Nottingham Road on the Midlands Meander make colourful garments and rugs (see pages 60 to 61).*

THE MIDLANDS – CREATIVE COUNTRYSIDE

Hilton • Howick Falls • Midmar Dam • Karkloof and Woodhouse Falls
Ecabazini Cultural Homestead • The Midlands Meander
Ixopo Buddhist Retreat

One of the prettiest parts of the country is the KwaZulu-Natal Midlands, an area of gently rolling hills through which you will pass after leaving Pietermaritzburg and heading north on the N3. The green, well-watered farmlands, lovely rivers and streams, and the indigenous and commercial forests have been a haven for rural and creative people since the early 1800s. The climate is markedly different from that of the coastal region – during the crispy cold autumns the leaves and grasslands turn burnt orange and yellow, and in spring and summer the hillsides are covered in carpets of green dotted with wild flowers.

The Midlands area is known for its small country inns nestled among dairy farms or against the backdrop of large pine plantations. It is here that you will also find some of the most spectacular waterfalls in the province, excellent fly-fishing waters, and a staggering variety of craft shops and home industries along a route known as the Midlands Meander. Residents from the bigger urban centres often enjoy a Sunday drive through the countryside, stopping off at a restaurant or coffee shop along the way.

Hilton

Just northwest of Pietermaritzburg on the N3 is the residential suburb of Hilton, with its atmosphere of a small country village. **Crossways,** a cosy little country inn in the village, is a favourite haunt of Pietermaritzburg's students and other locals, especially on a Sunday when lunch is served under the trees and umbrellas. Also in Hilton is the smart, mock-Tudor but delightfully atmospheric **Hilton Hotel,** conveniently set off the N3 highway. The hotel has two excellent restaurants, and log-fires in winter to welcome guests. Nearby is the Quarry Shopping Centre, built on the site of an old stone quarry.

Howick Falls

The first small town outside Pietermaritzburg (northwest along the N3) is Howick. It developed at a drift that crossed the Umgeni River, and although this drift provided the main crossing point of the Umgeni River, it was always rather treacherous. Numerous sad stories tell of people almost, or actually, being washed over the Howick Falls, as well as many tragic suicides. Over the years Howick has become famous for

ABOVE *One of the most popular venues on the Midlands Meander is Groundcover's old wood-and-iron settlers cottage, which has been converted into a quaint shop where handmade goods and leather shoes are sold.*

OPPOSITE TOP AND BOTTOM *The magnificent Howick Falls crash over a lip of rock into a large pool. The falls can be viewed from a platform at the top of the falls or, after a short hike, from the pools at the bottom.*

its 95-metre-high waterfall, known by the Zulus as *KwaNogqaza*, which means 'the place of the tall one'.

The falls lie close to the centre of the town, and a mere 200 metres from the edge of them is the bridge which crosses the Umgeni River into Howick. It was moved here from upstream in 1850 to make the route into town more direct, but by doing so, made it dangerous. The falls are magnificent to look at, especially during the rainy summer months, and a viewing platform, café, outdoor market and an information centre are located nearby. Those keen on hiking can follow a trail down to the pools at the bottom of the falls.

The Midlands – Creative Countryside

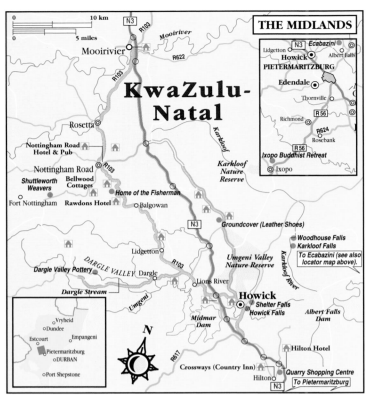

Midmar Dam

Further upstream from Howick, the Umgeni River has been dammed and the large man-made lake is known as Midmar Dam. The area around the dam has been declared a nature reserve and is run by the KwaZulu-Natal Nature Conservation Service. It is a popular spot for weekend picnicking, ski-boating, sailing, windsurfing and camping, and self-catering log cabins can also be rented. An annual event on the dam is the Midmar Mile, a swimming race which draws some 12 000 participants.

Karkloof and Woodhouse Falls

Only a short drive from Howick is another wonder of nature, the 105-metre-high Karkloof Falls. The main falls are said to take their name from the site of a wagon which overturned above the crossing (in Afrikaans, the word 'kar' refers to a cart or wagon and 'kloof' means cliff). The area around the falls is grassy and is a pleasant place to relax and enjoy a picnic.

A little further upstream are the Woodhouse Falls where there are braai spots and an ablution block. These falls are only 10 metres high, but, like the Karkloof and Howick falls, they've had their fair share of tragedies. The Woodhouse Falls were named after a young man who died while trying to ford the river on horseback.

OPPOSITE *The quiet waters of the Midmar Dam become a hive of activity during the popular Midmar Mile swimming race, which attracts some 12 000 participants year after year* (TOP), *and on weekends and during holidays when families come to enjoy sailing, water-skiing and fishing* (BOTTOM).

ABOVE *Places of natural beauty, such as the Karkloof Falls, abound in the Midlands.*

Fly-fishing

The trout waters of the Midlands are plentiful and well stocked.

The Drakensberg mountains are the source of many of KwaZulu-Natal's rivers, and during the rainy summer months, they cascade through the province's rolling hills. Much of the Midlands are farmlands and many of the rivers are dammed. They provide excellent opportunities for fly-fishing, and some farmers and hoteliers have stocked their dams with trout, fresh-water bass and other fish with this pleasant pursuit in mind. Many a good trout hole can also be found along the banks of rivers as they wind their way to the sea, particularly as you start moving out of the Midlands towards the Drakensberg.

Several very good guest houses, small hotels and country cottages along the Midlands Meander cater for the expert angler as well as the enthusiastic novice. Try Bellwood Cottages for self-catering, or Rawdons Hotel. Home of the Fisherman, a fly-fishing shop situated in the grounds of Rawdons, offers guided fly-fishing trips to the stocked dams, as well as fly-fishing clinics.

Rawdons Hotel near Nottingham Road is a tranquil haven for fly-fishing enthusiasts.

Ecabazini Cultural Homestead

On the outskirts of Pietermaritzburg, in the direction of the Albert Falls Dam, and with a view of the distant Karkloof Mountains, is a fascinating cultural village. The village is, in fact, a Zulu kraal, home to Cedric Hood, or 'CJ' as he is known, and a number of Zulu household members. CJ is considered by many people to be a 'white Zulu', a white man who has adopted the traditional customs and ways of the Zulu people. He opened Ecabazini Cultural Homestead to visitors who would like to learn about or experience Zulu culture. As there is no electricity, food is prepared over an open fire.

Part of a tour to the kraal includes a walk into the nearby fields to see how traditional crops such as *imfe* (yams), *amadumbi* (a type of potato) and *amabeca* (melons) are grown. It is possible to spend a night at the kraal, and **accommodation** is in authentic beehives homes or rondavels, with the emphasis being on preserving the traditional Zulu way of life.

The Midlands Meander

It would be easy to drive along the N3 freeway out of Howick and not realise that, just beyond the hills, a hive of artistic activity takes place. Approximately 120 arts and crafts studios, country hotels, flower farms, herb gardens, potters, weavers, leatherworkers and home-industry outlets are found along the Midlands Meander, which stretches north from Hilton to Mooi River, and from the Rietvlei in the east to the Dargle Valley in the west. Maps of this meander – which from humble beginnings has grown into the largest route of its kind in the country – are indispensable in order not to miss any of the unusual and interesting places worth visiting.

The area has been divided into four routes which can be enjoyed at any time of the year. During summer everything is lush and green, and during the winter the air is frosty – sometimes there is even snow – and welcoming fires are lit at the country inns.

The variety of items on sale is outstanding. As you drive through the pretty countryside, you can stop to buy beautifully handcrafted leather shoes at **Groundcover,** browse around the extensive range of stoneware, porcelain and terracotta at Ian

practice, and there are also excellent courses on bird-watching, relationships and ecology, all given from a Buddhist perspective. Month-long retreats are also possible, often when there is a visiting monk or teacher from outside the country. Most mornings begin very early with meditation and silence is usually observed for a set period. The setting is beautiful and the walks through the grasslands or the wooded areas peaceful. A massive and beautiful white *stupa* – a domed edifice around which people walk to meditate – overlooks the rolling foothills. The food is vegetarian and the accommodation comfortable, if somewhat austere.

Glenny's **Dargle Valley Pottery,** admire the exquisite hand-woven rugs, carpets and throws at **Shuttleworth Weaving,** shop for cotton bed-linen and honey, smoked trout and silk duvets, and much, much more, before stopping at a comfortable country inn such as the popular **Nottingham Road Hotel** for lunch or for the night.

The most rewarding way to see the area is by bicycle as most of the routes have tarred or good dirt roads. You do not need to be a fitness fanatic to enjoy a gentle cycle around the countryside, but if you want to ride on the longer gravel roads, you will probably need a fairly sturdy mountain bike.

Ixopo Buddhist Retreat
South Africa has a growing population of practising Buddhists, but you do not have to be one to spend time at the tranquil and friendly Ixopo Buddhist Retreat, situated to the southwest of Pietermaritzburg just outside the small village of Ixopo.

Throughout the year the retreat runs a variety of courses which anyone can attend. A weekend course in basic Buddhism will give you an outline of Buddhist philosophy and meditation

---

OPPOSITE TOP *The Nottingham Road Hotel is popular among local farmers and travellers for its excellent pub lunches.*

OPPOSITE BOTTOM *Shuttleworth Weaving on the Midlands Meander sells a variety of colourful handmade carpets, throws, jerseys and other items woven from wool as well as modern fibres.*

ABOVE *Also on the Midlands Meander, Groundcover has become synonymous with comfortable leather footwear.*

USEFUL INFORMATION
Crossways Country Inn: cnr Dennis Shepstone Drive and Old Howick Road, Hilton, tel. (033) 343-3267
Dargle Valley Pottery: off the D666 Dargle road, PO Box 820, Howick, 3290, tel./fax (033) 234-4377
Groundcover: off the Curry's Post road, PO Box 26, Nottingham Road, 3280, tel. (033) 330-6092, fax (033) 330-4694
Home of the Fisherman: Rawdons Hotel, Old Main Road, Nottingham Road, tel. (033) 263-6581, fax (033) 263-7195
Hilton Hotel: 1 Hilton Avenue, Hilton, tel. (033) 343-3311
Howick Publicity Association: opposite the Howick Falls viewing platform, PO Howick, 3290, tel. (033) 330-5305
Ixopo Buddhist Retreat: PO Box 131, Ixopo, 3276, tel. (0336) 34-1863
KwaZulu-Natal Nature Conservation Service: Queen Elizabeth Park, PO Box 13069, Cascades, Pietermaritzburg, 3202, tel. (033) 845-1999, fax (033) 845-1001, e-mail: bookings@rhino.org.za
Nottingham Road Hotel and Pub: PO Box 26, Nottingham Road, 3280, tel. (033) 263-6151, fax (033) 263-6167
Pietermaritzburg Tourism: Publicity House, 177 Commercial Road, Pietermaritzburg, tel. (033) 394-3535, e-mail: ppa@futurenet.co.za
Rawdons Hotel: Old Main Road, Nottingham Road, tel. (033) 263-6044, fax (033) 263-6048
Shuttleworth Weaving: 10 km from Nottingham Road on the Fort Nottingham road, PO Box 81, Nottingham Road, 3280, tel./fax (033) 263-6818
The Midlands Meander Committee: PO Box 874, Howick, 3290, tel. (033) 263-6008 or (033) 43-3664, e-mail: mm@futurenet.co.za, website: http\\www.midlandsmeander.org.za

Drakensberg –
The Dragon Mountains

LEFT *Snow covered and mirrored in the waters of the Tugela River, the Amphitheatre in the Royal Natal National Park is arguably one of the most impressive views of the entire Drakensberg range* (see *page 73*).

ABOVE *Hikers on their way up the mountain at Injasuti in the Giant's Castle Game Reserve walk past a Natal bottlebrush* (see *page 68*).

Drakensberg – The Dragon Mountains

Southern 'Berg · Central 'Berg · Northern 'Berg

Between KwaZulu-Natal and the Kingdom of Lesotho rises a great natural barrier, the mountain fortress of the Drakensberg range. This wilderness wonderland of colossal buttresses, montane forests, sheer cliffs, tumbling streams and deep valleys is a hiker's paradise. Black eagles and bearded vultures soar between the towering basalt cliffs, eland, oribi and rhebok wander through the sandstone-flanked valleys below, and, in the secret caves, many San (Bushman) paintings can still be found.

The Afrikaans trekkers called these mountains the Drakensberg – the Dragon Mountains. It is these mountains, purple and black, or swirling with mauve and blue clouds, that inspired the legendary South African-born author J.R.R. Tolkien when he wrote the classic Lord of the Rings. The Zulu people call them *uKhahlamba* – the Barrier of Spears – and for them it is a place of spirits and legendary monsters. Even the English names of the peaks and crevices are evocative: Giant's Castle, Champagne Castle, the Sentinel, the Amphitheatre, Monk's Cowl and Cathedral Peak.

The 'Berg, as it is affectionately known, is not a typical mountain range, stretching as it does some 1 600 kilometres from the country's northern provinces through to the Eastern Cape. The KwaZulu-Natal/Lesotho section is actually a continuation of the same escarpment that divides the highveld in the interior from the muggy malarial belt of the eastern coastal zone and lowveld. Some of the peaks in this region soar more than 3 000 metres.

Stretching from Bushman's Nek in the south to the Royal Natal National Park in the north, the wilderness areas that make up the Drakensberg National Park cover an area of some 243 000 hectares. A number of outdoor recreational opportunities are available for tourists, as well as a variety of accommodation, priced from budget to luxury. The park is administered by the KwaZulu-Natal Nature Conservation Services, and is divided into three main sections: the **southern, central** and **northern** 'Berg.

It is quite difficult to tour the 'Berg area in the traditional sense because the road system linking each area is fairly limited, requiring some circuitous routes to get from one place to another. It is better to choose one region, book in for a night or two and explore the immediate area.

In all sections of the park, the hiking trails are expertly laid out, good maps are available and campsites are situated at the start or end of most of the wilderness hikes. Thunderstorms and other extreme and often unpredictable weather conditions are common, and cautionary procedures should be followed when hiking in the area (a mountain register must be signed before setting off on a trail).

ABOVE *Cathkin Peak stands sentinel over the farmlands in the Drakensberg foothills.*

OPPOSITE *These thatched cottages provide a comfortable home base for hikers at Giant's Castle Game Reserve.*

At many of the nature reserves and campsites it is possible to hire horses, either for day or overnight rides into the wilderness areas. This is a spectacular way to enjoy the scenery, even if you have never ridden before. Mountain bikes are also allowed in some areas, as are four-wheel-drive vehicles, and trout-fishing opportunities abound.

Accommodation both in and outside the park is plentiful and varied, and ranges from rustic huts and caves for hikers to luxury resort-type hotels, and from campsites and bungalows to cosy B&Bs in private homes.

SOUTHERN 'BERG

To get to the southern 'Berg – the area between Bushman's Nek and Giant's Castle – take the N3 heading northwest out of Pietermaritzburg, and then the R617 turn-off at Merrivale. This will take you to the central village of Underberg from which you can access the various 'Berg resorts and trails. The National Hiking Way in the southern 'Berg has five mountain huts along its route, guided or unguided wilderness trails on foot, and guided horseback trails. Caves in this wilderness area provide overnight shelter for hikers, and fantastic examples of rock art can be seen. The Drakensberg Garden Hotel and the hotels at Bushman's Nek, all in the little 'Berg, as well as numerous self-catering cottages and B&Bs in the area, are within easy access of the beautiful **Garden Castle Nature Reserve**, which lies in the south of the Drakensberg National Park. Himeville and Underberg are the closest two villages, and it is through here that you must pass in order to reach Sani Pass (*see* page 67).

Also to be found in the southern region are **Cobham Nature Reserve, Loteni** and **Vergelegen**. Loteni is a popular trout-fishing spot which also has a small settlers' museum. These areas are the habitat of a diversity of birds, including black stork, lanner falcon, giant kingfisher, eagle and vulture, as well as numerous mammal species such as otter, mongoose, baboon, eland and a variety of other antelope.

Sani Pass

Named for the San (Bushmen) people who once inhabited the area, Sani Pass climbs to an altitude of 2 874 metres and is the only road link between KwaZulu-Natal and the rugged mountain tops of Lesotho. The 6,5-kilometre trip is usually undertaken in a four-wheel-drive vehicle, by motorbike or on foot, climbing approximately 1 330 metres. It is thrilling to stay overnight at the Sani Top Chalets on the edge of the escarpment. In winter, this part of the 'Berg is often covered in snow and it is a magical experience to wake up to a crisp morning in a white, winter wonderland. It is sometimes so cold that a couple of the frozen waterfalls on the pass do not melt between May and September. To get to the top of Sani Pass, you have to pass through the Lesotho border posts and so need to carry the necessary documentation.

OPPOSITE TOP *Loteni Nature Reserve has a campsite as well as self-catering thatched huts tucked away in the mountains.*

OPPOSITE CENTRE *A wonderful way to enjoy the 'Berg is on horseback. There are a number of bridle trails to choose from, such as this one at Cobham Nature Reserve.*

OPPOSITE BOTTOM *Quiet fishing spots abound in the Drakensberg foothills, such as at Lake Navarone in the southern 'Berg.*

Splashy Fen

An annual event in the Drakensberg foothills which should not be missed is the Splashy Fen Music Festival. What started as a small get-together of musicians for a few days of 'jamming' on Splashy Fen farm near Bushman's Nek has grown into a 'Woodstock-like' festival of contemporary music. Every year during April/May, performances take place in various marquees and open-air 'amphitheatres', and there is a folk-club free stage and craft market. Although accommodation is available at guest houses and B&Bs in the area, most people camp with their families at the river or on the surrounding hillsides. A classical 'Splashy' also takes place some time during September every year, featuring philharmonic orchestras, string quartets and others.

Crowds flock to the annual Splashy Fen folk music festival in the Drakensberg foothills.

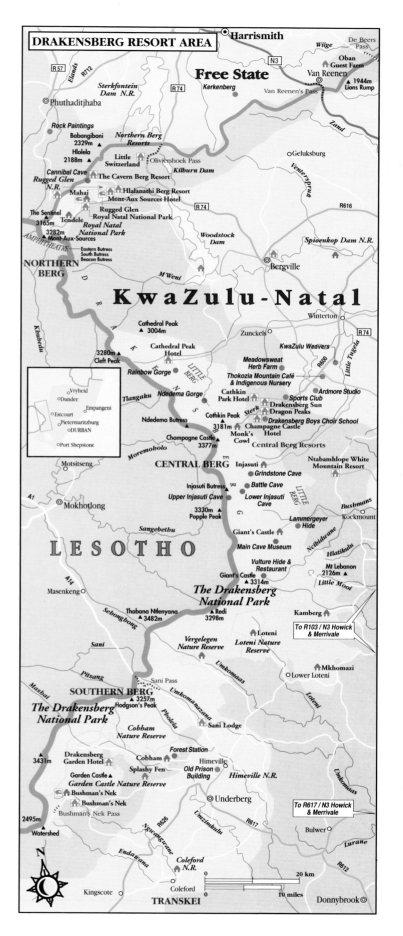

CENTRAL 'BERG

The quickest ways to the central 'Berg district are via the N3, taking the Mooi River toll plaza exit, the Central 'Berg/Giant's Castle exit near Estcourt, or the R74 Winterton exit.

Kamberg and Giant's Castle roughly link the southern to the central region, which is by far the busiest and most popular section of the Drakensberg. It is in the central 'Berg that you will find **Injasuti, Cathkin Peak, Monk's Cowl, Champagne Castle, Cathedral Peak** and the beautiful **Ndedema Gorge.**

Giant's Castle is where the **Lammergeier Hide** and **Vulture Restaurant,** set high on a cliff, give bird-watchers an opportunity to observe the endangered bearded vulture, known locally as the lammergeier ('lamb-killer'). This name was given by Afrikaans farmers who erroneously believed that the birds killed their young livestock. The hide takes a maximum of six people and advance booking is necessary. In the mornings, between May and September, game rangers put out meat and bones for the birds. Visitors are taken to the hide by vehicle but have to make their way back to camp on foot. Besides the lammergeier, you are also likely to see lanner falcon, jackal buzzard, Cape vulture and black eagle.

Two wilderness experiences are offered in the Giant's Castle Reserve. One is a three-day, two-night walk crossing sparkling rivers below the towering peaks of the mountains. The other is a horseback trail, which can stretch from two to three nights. Overnight accommodation is in cosy caves. The trails season is between September and May as the icy 'Berg winter conditions make it dangerous and sometimes impossible to hike during the months of June, July or August.

The Giant's Castle region boasts several kilometres of trout waters, but one of the principal attractions remains the superb rock art in the **Main Caves** (*see* Rock Art, page 70). Injasuti has three caves: **Lower**

Opposite top During the cold Drakensberg winters, Monk's Cowl and Cathkin Peak are often covered in snow, turning the landscape into a white wonderland of icy crystals.

Opposite centre and bottom left Carcasses are put out to attract the endangered bearded vulture, or lammergeier, to the Vulture Restaurant in the Giant's Castle area (Centre bottom and bottom left). Also seen here is a black eagle (Centre top) taking off from the 'restaurant'.

Opposite bottom right The little stone hut on the Giant's Cup hiking trail provides overnight shelter for hikers.

Top Traditional Zulu settlements dot the fertile, grassy foothills in the Injasuti district.

Below The natural beauty of the Mlambonja wilderness area creates a dramatic backdrop in the Cathedral Peak region of the central Drakensberg.

Injasuti, Upper Injasuti and **Grindstone** caves, which can be booked as overnight stops for hikers. Besides the caves, Injasuti also has a little hutted camp surrounded by magnificent scenery and fine examples of rock paintings at **Battle Cave.** The river running through this spectacular valley offers some of the best natural jacuzzis and water slides in the Drakensberg.

Accessed from the Cathedral Peak section of the central 'Berg, **Rainbow Gorge** is an easy walk from the Cathedral Peak Hotel through a beautiful yellowwood forest. The gorge fills with little rainbows caused by the fine spray of the many small waterfalls cascading down into the gorge. The further into the gorge, the wetter the walk, as one has to cross the river a number of times to get around boulders that crashed down hundreds of years ago, lodging between the sandstone sides of the ravine.

Along the R600 stretch of road leading from Winterton to the central 'Berg reserves are numerous well-known resort hotels which cater for families on holiday. They include places such as Champagne Valley, The Nest, Dragon Peaks, Cayley Lodge and the Drakensberg Sun.

Rock Art

The small indigenous people of southern Africa, known as the San or Bushmen, once inhabited the beautiful wilderness now called the Drakensberg National Park, and evidence of their stay is found in the thousands of examples of rock paintings they left behind.

For more than 40 years, people have been searching for their paintings in the Drakensberg and, during this time, some 22 000 individually painted images have been discovered and recorded. Some of the rock shelters have more than a thousand paintings on them. They are mainly of people and their equipment, of animals and often of what appears to be hunting and spiritual activities. Some paintings of wagons and horses are obviously more recent, having been done during the colonial period. The age of the paintings remains largely unknown, but it is believed that San hunter-gatherers lived in the Drakensberg from about 8 000 years ago until the 1800s. The last recorded sighting of the Drakensberg San was by a honeymoon couple in the 1870s.

Many of the rock art sites are not open to the general public, mainly because over the years they have been defaced or vandalised by thoughtless visitors, who have thereby destroyed some of the last reminders of Stone Age hunter-gatherer life in the area. However, there are still a number of fascinating sites that are open and can be viewed.

Some of the more interesting and important San painting sites are found at **Main Caves** in the Giant's Castle Game Reserve. More than 500 paintings – some now barely discernible – can be viewed on two massive rock overhangs. The eland, the largest of the antelopes which can still be found in the Drakensberg,

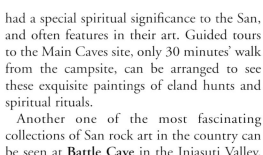

had a special spiritual significance to the San, and often features in their art. Guided tours to the Main Caves site, only 30 minutes' walk from the campsite, can be arranged to see these exquisite paintings of eland hunts and spiritual rituals.

Another one of the most fascinating collections of San rock art in the country can be seen at **Battle Cave** in the Injasuti Valley. While this cave has some 750 paintings on the rock walls, it is not the quantity but the content that is so interesting. One vignette depicts a red monochrome scene of two feuding San groups, and it is from this that the cave gets its name. This is also one of the few places in the Drakensberg to feature depictions of lion. The site can only be visited by those joining a guided walk from the Injasuti Hutted Camp.

The paintings in **Cannibal Caves** in the south/central 'Berg are faint and not as interesting as some of the others, but the cave itself has a lively history. Apparently during the mid-nineteenth century, a group of cannibals (not of San origin) lived in the caves, roaming the area of present-day Lesotho, marauding and attacking lone travellers. Their victims were strung up in the cave to keep them fresh for eating. Rumour has it that, when 'food' was in short supply, the cannibals bartered and ate their own wives and children.

ABOVE AND BELOW *The Drakensberg is one of the richest areas of San rock art in the world, boasting approximately 500 sites and more than 22 000 paintings. Shown here are some excellent examples from the game pass shelter in the Kamberg region.*

OPPOSITE TOP *When the clouds lift off the face of the Drakensberg, the magnificent Cathedral Peak and Champagne Castle tower above the farmlands of Champagne Valley.*

OPPOSITE BOTTOM *Traditional crafts made by the local Zulu women are sold alongside the road in Champagne Valley.*

The Mountain Meander

A meander through Champagne Valley will take you to a number of artists' studios, craft shops, tea gardens and restaurants. Start at Winterton village with its small but interesting museum (*see* below), and wind your way along the R600.

Thokozia Mountain Café and Indigenous Nursery, a nursery attached to a pleasant little coffee shop, is situated at the main crossroads and turn-off to the 'Berg resorts. **Meadowsweet Herb Farm,** signposted further along the R600, grew from humble beginnings to become a main supplier of herbs to restaurants and grocery stores around the country. All sorts of farm goodies can be bought at the farm shop on the premises. **KwaZulu Weavers** lies along the road between Winterton and the crossroads, and is a small shop where beautiful rugs and throws are woven. Also on the Mountain Meander is **Ardmore Studio,** a must for anyone interested in ceramics (*see* page 72).

Winterton Museum

Just off the main street of Winterton is a delightful museum that is certainly worth a visit. It portrays the living history of the people in the area. Residents from the Early and Late Stone Age and the Early and Late Iron Age periods are represented, as are the groups who fled from Shaka's invading armies during the period known as the *Mfecane* (the 'crushing') and the first white settlers, the Voortrekkers and English. Many of the locals have contributed family heirlooms to the museum.

Using materials collected in the way their ancestors did, the local Ngwane people have built grass huts next to the little wood and iron structure which houses both the museum and the library. Farmers in the district have donated old farm implements and other items used by their pioneering forefathers. Of great interest is a display of photographs of San rock art, and, if you are planning a hike into the mountains to see rock paintings, first take a look at this '**San Art Gallery**', consisting of 10 panels of 180 photographs.

Bringing the exhibit into the present day is a small but poignant display of the actual voting booths, UV-detectors and banners used by the Winterton community during South Africa's historic first democratic elections in 1994, as well as a few photographs of the locals queuing to vote. Outside there is a curious wooden 'caravan', built in 1918 by an eccentric local, Maximillian John Ludwick Weston, in which he drove his family across Africa to tour Europe, before returning to settle in the Bergville district in 1933.

Ardmore Studio

Situated on a road off the R600 in the Champagne Valley area is Ardmore farm, once the home of internationally acclaimed ceramic artist Fee Halstead-Berning and her protégée, Bonnie Ntshanlitshali. Although Fee and her family no longer live here, she still operates the Ardmore Studio and her home is now a guest house. This rural studio and gallery, established in the old stone stables on this farm in the foothills of the Drakensberg, is probably one of the most unusual and interesting ceramics studios you will find in the country.

Women from the surrounding rural farmlands work here, creating their often fun, sometimes functional artworks, which reflect a uniquely naïve perspective of the world. Guided by Fee, the women's work has received international acclaim and

is exhibited in galleries around the world. The artists work together in the true communal fashion of Africa, some working in clay, others painting while another glazes, and it is a delight to wander around the studio while they are busy. The work is all highly original and colourful, and, while it is in no way 'traditional', it is unmistakably African. Zebras race around the lip of a teapot, lizards scamper and butterflies flutter over dinner plates, and black saints, arms outstretched, proclaim words of wisdom, while giraffes festooned with birds become the handles of cups and jugs. For day visitors to Ardmore, the guest house provides tea and scones under the trees, with the Drakensberg range as a stunning backdrop.

ABOVE *Ardmore Studio in the Champagne Valley is well known for its beautifully painted ceramics that are also highly original.*

OPPOSITE TOP *The mighty Tugela River thunders down the escarpment from its source high up in the Drakensberg mountains.*

OPPOSITE BOTTOM LEFT *The lovely pink* Hesperantha coccinea *is one of many wild flowers that can be found in the Drakensberg.*

OPPOSITE BOTTOM RIGHT *The Sentinel Chain Ladder is bolted onto the rock face, providing one of the more exciting descents for hikers coming down from the Amphitheatre.*

Drakensberg Boys' Choir

It may seem odd to find one of the world's foremost choir schools located in such a remote rural community. But, no doubt, it is from the majestic peaks of Champagne Castle and Cathkin Peak, in whose shadow the school nestles, that the boys draw their inspiration. The Drakensberg Boys' Choir is often mentioned in the same breath as the Vienna and the Harlem boys' choirs, and their concerts are not to be missed.

They regularly undertake local and international concert tours. The school has a beautiful theatre and, every Wednesday afternoon during term time, there is a performance to which members of the public are invited. Details of other scheduled evening performances can be obtained from the school. Choirs may not normally appeal to you, but, if you would like to hear foot-stomping, spirit-rousing and sometimes lump-in-the-throat African music, look out for concerts where the boys sing indigenous music. The Music in the Mountains Festival takes place during April/May every year, and their magnificent Christmas concerts are also not to be missed. The school is located about 17 kilometres from the R600 crossroads near Winterton.

Members of the world-famous Drakensberg Boys' Choir.

NORTHERN 'BERG

Access to the Royal Natal National Park is along the R74 off the N3, passing through the little village of Bergville. The focus of the park is undoubtedly the magnificent sheer basalt rock face known as **the Amphitheatre**, a wall of rock measuring more than 2 900 metres high and 4 kilometres across between the

3 047-metre-high Eastern Buttress, the 3 121-metre-high South and Beacon buttresses, and **the Sentinel** in the north, which stands 3 165 metres high. Over a section of this mighty wall, called **Mont-Aux-Sources**, the Tugela River plunges more than 1 000 metres off the plateau in a series of five dramatic waterfalls into the gorge below.

Again, the most popular activity enjoyed by visitors to this area is walking and hiking, and the 6-hour hike to the bottom of the Amphitheatre is a must.

Drakensberg – The Dragon Mountains

Eastern Buttress 3 047 m ⬇

⬇ Devil's Tooth 3 044 m

THE AMPHITHEATRE

The Sentinel 3 165 m ➡

Beacon Buttress 3 121 m ⬇

Mont-Aux-Sources Peak 3 282 m ⬇

Tugela Waterfall ⬇

This pleasant walk passes through a natural tunnel and winds across the river and back a number of times along the route.

Accommodation in the park is offered at **Tendele Hutted Camp**, which is situated in one of the most picturesque of all the 'Berg settings, with each bungalow affording a view of the Amphitheatre. **Tendele Lodge** also has superb views and a large fireplace for the icy winter months. **Mahai Campground**, a large campsite at the foot of the range, caters for 400 campers among exotic big trees, while the nearby **Rugged Glen Campsite** around the mountainside is much smaller and perhaps more intimate.

OPPOSITE *One of the most scenic walks in the Royal Natal National Park leads to the Cascades.*

TOP *Tendele Camp in the Royal Natal National Park has an unsurpassed view of the Amphitheatre.*

RIGHT *Hiking is undoubtedly one of the most popular ways to experience the natural beauty of the 'Berg.*

USEFUL INFORMATION

The main KwaZulu-Natal Tourism office, situated at the Tourist Junction in Durban, includes bodies such as the KwaZulu-Natal Nature Conservation Service and many other tour operators who will be able to provide information on the Drakensberg. Bookings and enquiries about accommodation, the vulture restaurant, rock art and hikes can be made through the KwaZulu-Natal Nature Conservation Service's office here, or at their Pietermaritzburg head office. Bookings for other resorts can also be made here, or through the Drakensberg Tourism Association.

Ardmore Guest Farm and Ceramic Art Studio: PO Box 1005, Winterton, 3340, tel./fax (036) 468-1314
Drakensberg Boys' Choir: Private Bag X20, Winterton, 3340, tel. (036) 468-1012, fax (036) 468-1709
Drakensberg Tourism Association: PO Box 325, Bergville, 3350, tel./fax (036) 448-1557
KwaZulu-Natal Nature Conservation Service: PO Box 13069, Cascades, 3202, tel. (033) 845-1000, fax (033) 845-1001, e-mail: bookings@rhino.org.za

KwaZulu-Natal Tourism: Tourist Junction, 160 Pine Street, Durban, tel. (031) 304-7144, fax (031) 305-6693, e-mail: tkzn@iafrica.com
KwaZulu Weavers: PO Box 1066, Cedarwood Village, Winterton, 3340, tel. (036) 488-1098/1657
Meadowsweet Farm Organic Herbs: on the D184 road which turns off the R600 road, Champagne Valley, PO Box 193, Winterton, 3340, tel./fax (036) 468-1216
Mountain Meander: PO Box 1005, Winterton, 3340, tel. (036) 468-1314, website: http\\www.drakensbergmeander.co.za
Sani Top Chalets: PO Box 169, Himeville, 3256, tel./fax (033) 702-1320, e-mail: drakensberg.info@futurenet.org.za
Thokozia Mountain Café and Indigenous Nursery: off R600, Champagne Valley, PO Box 378, Winterton, 3340, tel./fax (036) 488-1273
Winterton Museum: Church Street, Winterton, tel. (036) 488-1620
Splashy Fen: tel. (031) 572-3073, fax (031) 572-4909, e-mail: bartf@saol.com, website: http\\www.splashyfen.co.za

South & North Coast –
Sea, Sun & Surf

LEFT *The warm climate and safe beaches, such as Compensation Beach at Ballito Bay on the North Coast, make KwaZulu-Natal's coastline an ideal holiday destination for locals and foreigners alike.*

ABOVE *Paddle-skiing is just one of the many water sports enjoyed along the province's coast.*

SOUTH & NORTH COAST – SEA, SUN & SURF

South Coast • North Coast

KwaZulu-Natal has always been synonymous with sunny beaches and warm seas, and the coast south of Durban is where many people have gone to enjoy these appealing aspects of the province. Over the years it has grown into one long holiday resort, with blocks of flats, holiday apartments, hotels and guest houses popping up everywhere. As one of the country's premier domestic tourist markets, the South Coast is usually busy during national holiday seasons, but, out of season, it is the perfect place for a quiet beach holiday.

All along the coast, from Amanzimtoti just outside Durban to Port Edward on the border of the Eastern Cape, small villages and coastal towns offer visitors plenty of opportunities for swimming, surfing and various other water sports. The fishing is excellent, from the beaches and the rocks, as well as from offshore, and there are several launch sites for ski-boats.

The North Coast, on the other hand, has not developed at the same pace, although some villages have grown substantially in recent years. The drive north out of Durban along the coastal road takes you through fields of waving sugar cane, patches of dark-green coastal forest and in-between, small holiday villages set against the Indian Ocean. Until recently, a big freeway by-passed many of the North Coast villages, but it now extends southwards as well, making it possible to travel from the far northern coast of the province to the south, seldom passing through a town. This is both a blessing and a curse. It means that traffic congestion is lessened, but it also means that it is easy for visitors to bypass some of the pretty towns along the coast.

Part of the North Coast is known as the Dolphin Coast and includes places such as Ballito Bay, Shaka's Rock, Salt Rock, Sheffield and Umhlali.

THE SOUTH COAST

Driving out of Durban south along the coast, the first town you pass is **Amanzimtoti.** Despite the high-rise buildings and busy roads, this holiday resort is popular among local tourists for its fine beaches. The coast from here southwards to **Umkomaas** is less developed because the area used to fall under the old KwaZulu government during the apartheid years. The land is

ABOVE *As you wind your way down the South Coast, the landscape is dominated by rolling hills of sugar cane – one of the province's primary crops.*

OPPOSITE TOP LEFT *The Umnini craft centre near Umgababa on the South Coast is one of the many roadside craft centres where traditional crafts and other curios are sold.*

OPPOSITE TOP RIGHT *The Uvongo River plunges down a narrow gorge just before it reaches the little lagoon at the popular beach resort of the same name.*

OPPOSITE BOTTOM *Not all the South Coast beaches are packed with sun-worshippers. There are still a few lovely, unspoilt areas where a solitary walk can be enjoyed.*

still administered by the tribal authorities, and it is interesting to see the hundreds of homesteads dotting the hills along this pretty stretch of coastline. The further south you travel, the less populated the region becomes, until you reach **Scottburgh**, whereafter there is a string of coastal villages such as **Park Rynie, Kelso, Pennington, Sezela, Hibberdene** and **Sea Park**.

Port Shepstone marks the division between what is considered to be the South Coast and the lower South Coast. From here, subtle changes in climate and vegetation occur.

South of the Mzimkulu River, which reaches the sea at Port Shepstone, are a succession of sandy bays, rocky outcrops and river estuaries. The area's sunny summers and protected beaches make it popular among tourists, who flock here during holiday seasons. One of the most popular resorts is **Uvongo**, a place named for a small, beautiful river, the iVungu. It tumbles down a 23-metre-high waterfall into a 27-metre-deep pool and then flows out into a lagoon, the deepest in KwaZulu-Natal.

South & North Coast – Sea, Sun & Surf

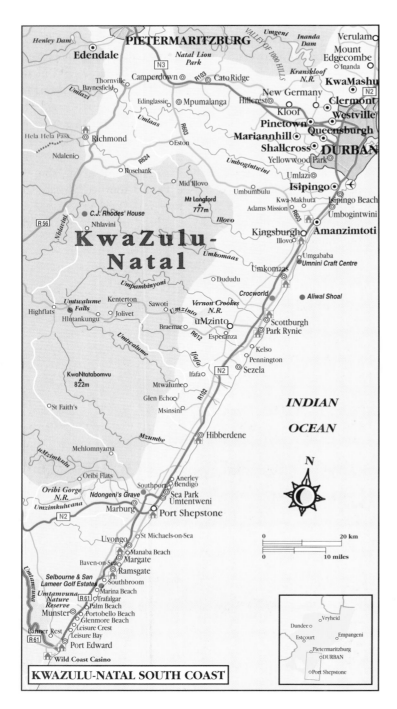

KWAZULU-NATAL SOUTH COAST

The nearby resorts of **St Michael's-on-Sea** and **Manaba Beach,** with their safe beaches, tidal pools and excellent fishing spots, draw thousands of holiday-makers year after year. A little further down the coast is the busy commercial centre of **Margate,** which has grown rapidly in recent years. It developed around a lovely sandy beach and a small lagoon that provide recreational opportunities such as boating and canoeing, and it is also a favourite surfing spot. A spectacular air show is held annually at the Margate airfield, drawing crowds from around the country.

Other holiday towns along the lower South Coast include **Ramsgate, Southbroom, Marina Beach** and **Port Edward,** all with safe beaches and life guards on duty in the holiday season.

The South Coast effectively ends at the Umtamvuna River, which is spanned by an elegant metal bridge leading into the Eastern Cape. The Umtamvuna begins inland, cutting a spectacular gorge through to the sea. On the southern side of the river, at its mouth, lies the **Wild Coast Casino.** Paddle boats, canoes, jet-skis and skiboats belonging to the casino or to holiday-makers make use of the lower section of the river, but, further up, it becomes a little quieter, with only a few small jetties from which anglers cast their lines.

Golf

The South Coast is fast growing into a golf haven of note. No fewer than nine excellent 18-hole golf courses, two 9-hole courses and a driving range lie within a short distance of Margate, one of the main centres midway along the coast. **Selbourne Estate**, just past Scottburgh, **San Lameer**, between Margate and Port Edward, and the **Wild Coast Casino** (which is actually in the Eastern Cape) near Port Edward are three golf estates with spectacular greens and views of the sea and indigenous coastal forests.

Along the North Coast are a number of first-class country clubs, such as the **Umhlali Country Club**, where you can play tennis, squash and golf. **Zimbali Lodge**, about 3 kilometres north of Ballito, is an upmarket golf estate that combines both an African and colonial atmosphere. It has become popular, not only because of its superb greens, designed by renowned American Tom Weiskopf, but also because of its wonderful setting and outstanding service.

Diving on Aliwal Shoal

Two of the main scuba-diving spots on the KwaZulu-Natal coast are Sodwana Bay (*see* page 130) and Aliwal Shoal, a reef that lies offshore of Umkomaas. Out of season, Umkomaas is a sleepy little coastal village and, if two or more fishermen are seen on the beach, it is a lot. But, during weekends and holiday seasons, Umkomaas beach is packed as dive operators set up their shade-cloth covers, umbrellas and billboards, and divers squeeze into their wetsuits and check their tanks. Ski-boats hover in the shore-break waiting to launch through the surf to take divers out to sea, and four-wheel-drive vehicles used for launching park nose to tail along the length of the beach.

Besides Aliwal Shoal's spectacular corals, tropical fish, octopus, turtles and other marine life, one of the most exciting aspects about diving there is the possibility of seeing sharks. This is an excellent place to see ragged-toothed sharks, or 'raggies', as they are commonly known, with their heavy, pointed snouts and formidable teeth. They generally reach approximately 3 metres in length, although, on the odd

OPPOSITE TOP *The resort town of Margate is a hub of activity, providing good surf, good fishing and safe swimming.*

OPPOSITE BOTTOM *Gambling is not the only thing to do at the Wild Coast Hotel and Casino. Horse rides, golf, water-sporting activities and quiet walks along the beach can also be enjoyed.*

BELOW *Aliwal Shoal off Umkomaas is one of the country's premier dive spots and a great place to see ragged-tooth sharks as well as a variety of other colourful sea-life.*

occasion, 5-metre-long sharks are still seen off the shoal. Other species that divers may encounter off the reef are Zambezi, blue, dusky and hammerhead sharks.

Even though sharks are considered dangerous and should be treated with the utmost respect, few unpleasant incidents have been reported off Aliwal Shoal. Professional dive operators are experienced and give all the guidance needed underwater for dealing with these fascinating beasts. Many sharks are tagged for identification and further study as part of an ongoing research programme, and divers often report with excitement that they were fortunate enough to have spotted one of these specimens in the blue depths of the ocean.

Crocworld

A number of crocodile farms occur along both the North Coast and South Coast, each offering much the same services: a tour of the pools, watching feeding time, curio shops and sometimes a little coffee shop. However, Scottburgh's Crocworld is not only the largest crocodile 'farm' in the country, but it is also the biggest on the African continent. It is home to more than 10 000 crocodiles and to a crocodile aquarium, and houses various tanks where the antics of large, reptilian water monitors, tigerfish and catfish can be viewed.

Feeding time is a wonderful opportunity to witness the fearsome crocodiles close up, snatching with their powerful jaws at the meat thrown to them. Crocodiles are carnivorous and in the wild their diet ranges from fish and water birds to small mammals. But they have been known to catch much larger animals from river banks. If the prey proves to be too bulky to swallow in one go, the crocodile drags it under water, rotating it rapidly until a manageable chunk of meat is torn free.

The crocodiles at Crocworld vary in size from hatchlings to enormous adults, seemingly lethargic amphibians basking on the sand. But do not be fooled – these reptiles are exceedingly quick and agile when they need to be. Crocodiles are among the oldest living relatives of the long-extinct dinosaurs, an order that ruled the earth some 225 million to 65 million years ago. In reptilian terms, the crocodile's brain is apparently reasonably well developed, and, when raised in captivity, they have been known to display some surprisingly advanced behaviour. For instance, they adapt well to established routines, and, in some instances, can relate to humans in a modest way, recognising their keepers and even tolerating a certain amount of handling.

Crocodiles are not the only animals you can view at Crocworld. Walkways and viewing bridges lead you through the park, which is landscaped with indigenous trees and other plants, to large **breeding dams,** home to more than 300 adult crocodiles. The dams attract a wide variety of birds, including plovers, water dikkops and comical hamerkops, and you could also catch a glimpse of the resident fish eagles, jackal buzzards and flamingos. In the surrounding thickets live shy bushbabies and cheeky vervet monkeys.

A **guided tour** around Crocworld will give you an in-depth idea of the crocodile farming business, from the methods of farming to skinning and meat processing. Crocodiles are prized for the fine leather they yield, and also for their meat – making them a lucrative agricultural product farmed intensively in

ABOVE AND LEFT *Crocodiles, which once inhabited many of the rivers in this part of the country, can now be viewed from a safe distance at Crocworld near Scottburgh, as well as at some of the other crocodile farms in KwaZulu-Natal. The Nile crocodiles at Crocworld range in size from tiny little hatchlings to enormous adults.*

OPPOSITE *The holiday town of Margate is a popular fishing spot for ski-boaters and shore-anglers alike. Here anglers can be seen casting their lines into the surf from the pier at the main beach.*

many parts of southern Africa. In addition to the guided tour, or as an alternative, a lovely 3-kilometre **nature trail** takes you through typical KwaZulu-Natal coastal bush, which offers more opportunities to see birds, monkeys and small antelope.

Also at Crocworld is a conference centre, an education centre screening video presentations, several natural history exhibits, a children's playground, bunny park and a farmyard. The **tea garden** serves tea and scones, and, for more adventurous diners, the **restaurant** offers crocodile steaks and kebabs. The **curio shop** sells, among other things, crocodile-skin bags, purses and belts, as well as takeaway crocodile steaks and biltong.

Sardine Fever

During the balmy summer months, the South Coast usually experiences a mass influx of visitors to its coastline, but during winter, generally around July, people flock here for another reason: to witness the annual 'sardine run'. Few things can match the thrill of this incredible natural phenomenon, which occurs nowhere else in the world.

Countless millions of sardines migrate northwards up the coast in gigantic shoals, followed by enormous game fish, sea birds and frenzied anglers. The rare occasions when a massive shoal beaches itself are events of great excitement. People dash into the shallow water with buckets, basins, nets or anything they can lay their hands on to try to gather up the thrashing fish, and women have even been seen wading into the water, scooping up sardines in their skirts.

For a few weeks each year, the roads are busy with spectators and boat-towing vehicles, and the sea is filled with ski-boat fishermen following the shoals in the hopes of landing some of the ever-present game fish that accompany them. Apart from the fact that this fascinating event provides local communities with a plentiful harvest of food, it has also become a major tourist attraction, bringing visitors to the South Coast from all over the world.

Oribi Gorge Nature Reserve

The entrance to the Oribi Gorge Nature Reserve is about 21 kilometres from Port Shepstone on the Kokstad road, marked by the KwaZulu-Natal Nature Conservation Service logo. Formed by the Umzimkulwana River, Oribi Gorge is a nature lover's dream. Wonderful walks and self-guided trails lead down into the gorge, and, although there is no big game, there are plenty of bushbuck, common reedbuck and grey and blue duiker to be seen, as well as a great diversity of birdlife.

A favourite place for hikers to climb to is the aptly named Camel Rock, an overhanging rock that reaches out over the sheer cliff face of the gorge. The **campsite** at the nature reserve is perfectly situated at the head of the Umzimkulwana Gorge, commanding an extensive view of Oribi Gorge. Accommodation is also available in **self-catering huts**.

ABOVE AND RIGHT *The South Coast boasts many places of spectacular natural beauty, such as Oribi Gorge, which was formed by the Umzimkulwana River cutting through massive rocks thousands of years ago. The sheer cliffs provide wonderful opportunities for adventure sports such as abseiling.*

OPPOSITE TOP *Ballito Bay has grown from a small fishing village to one of the most popular resort towns on the North Coast.*

OPPOSITE BOTTOM *Roadside traders sell a variety of tropical fruit such as bananas, pawpaws, avocado pears and pineapples as well as traditional crops such as sweet potatoes and the small, hairy, potato-like* mdumbes.

Umtamvuna Nature Reserve

The southernmost reserve in KwaZulu-Natal, the Umtamvuna Nature Reserve consists of riverine forests and steep cliffs plunging down towards the river. A number of **trails** can be followed, all offering splendid scenery as well as an astonishing variety of trees, shrubs and other plants of botanical interest. Few people are aware that three of the world's centres of plant diversity (CPDs) lie within the KwaZulu-Natal/Eastern Cape region, where the Umtamvuna Reserve is situated. CPDs are areas of global botanical importance, containing diverse and large numbers of endemic or threatened species of social, economic, cultural or scientific importance.

To get to the reserve, follow the N2 south to Port Edward. At the Port Edward crossroads, turn right and drive along the Izingolweni road for approximately 8 kilometres. The entrance to the reserve is signposted on your left.

THE NORTH COAST

Heading north out of Durban are two main roads: the N2 toll-road and the old North Coast road. The latter winds along the coast, through small villages and fields of undulating sugar cane on its way to Zululand. As you travel further north, the coast and countryside open out, and the towns and villages become fewer. The beaches are not as protected as the South Coast beaches, but are uncluttered and stretch for miles and miles.

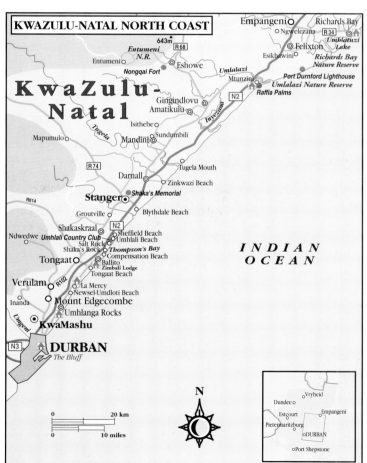

87

Tongaat, Mount Edgcombe and Verulam are all associated with the sugar industry, while Umdloti, Tongaat Beach, Umhlali, Ballito, Salt Rock, Shaka's Rock and Thompson's Bay are popular as beach holiday resorts – although not on the same scale as the South Coast towns. Ballito, which is about 25 minutes' drive from Durban, offers ideal bathing facilities and a number of good small hotels and guest houses.

Fishing is excellent along the North Coast, with numerous spots that are popular for rock and ski-boat fishing. Richards Bay is a fast-growing industrial centre with a busy port connected by railway lines to the mines of the hinterland.

Several major industries, such as Alusaf, a massive aluminium reduction plant, Indian Ocean Fertilizer, and Richards Bay Minerals, which mines heavy sands both north and south of the bay, have been established in Richards Bay. However, they do not detract from the lovely beaches and the good fishing, both in the harbour and along the coast.

Mtunzini and the Umlalazi Nature Reserve

The village of Mtunzini, which in Zulu means 'place of shade', is probably the only place, other than Kosi Bay in the far north of the province (*see* page 133), where you will see such a magnificent stand of giant raffia palms. The **Raffia Palm Monument** has a walkway through the raffia palm grove, where some of the trees are 25 metres high. This is also probably one

of the few opportunities to see palm nut vultures, which only live in the vicinity of raffia palms, feeding on the palm nuts.

The Umlalazi Nature Reserve takes its name from the nearby river – in Zulu, the *Mlalazi* or 'place of whetstones'. The small, 908-hectare reserve lies about 1,5 kilometres east of Mtunzini and includes pleasant coastal dune forest and swampland. Numerous small mammals, such as bushbuck, blue and grey duiker and reedbuck, and a variety of birds can be seen. A few crocodile still live in parts of the river. A short **trail** leads through the mangroves, which grow on the small islands and on the banks of the lagoon, and the reserve also has a few longer trails and good picnic sites. A **campsite** and a few **chalets** are available for overnight stays.

OPPOSITE TOP LEFT *The pedestrian walkway along the edge of the ocean at Umdloti Beach makes it easy for the elderly and other walkers to get close to the sea.*

OPPOSITE TOP RIGHT *Although not indigenous, the hibiscus flower proliferates in the warm tropical climate of the coastal areas.*

OPPOSITE BOTTOM *Shaka's Rock on the North Coast draws visitors to its safe and secluded swimming beach.*

ABOVE *The North Coast beaches are more remote and undeveloped than those in the south. From Mtunzini the coast stretches in long, lonely beaches all the way to Kosi Bay near Mozambique.*

USEFUL INFORMATION

Aliwal Shoal Scuba-diving Expeditions: Andy Cobb Eco Diving, 10 Marion Road, St Winifreds, 4126, tel. (031) 916-4239

Crocworld: Old South Coast Road, Scottburgh, tel. (039) 976-1103

Dolphin Coast Publicity (North Coast): PO Box 534, Ballito, 4420, tel./fax (032) 946-1997, e-mail: info@dolphincoast.co.za

KwaZulu-Natal Nature Conservation Service: PO Box 13069, Cascades, 3202, tel. (033) 845-1000, fax (033) 845-1001

KwaZulu-Natal Tourism: Tourist Junction, 160 Pine Street, Durban, tel. (031) 304-7144, fax (031) 305-6693, e-mail: tkzn@iafrica.com

Mtunzini Publicity: PO Box 24, Mtunzini, 3867, tel. (035) 340-1421, fax (035) 340-1847

Oribi Gorge Nature Reserve: PO Box 81, Paddock, 4244, tel. (039) 679-1644 (or contact the KwaZulu-Natal Nature Conservation Service for reservations)

Port Shepstone Publicity: PO Box 2523, Port Shepstone, 4240, tel. (039) 682-2455, fax (039) 682-5003, e-mail: sheppie@ps.lia.net

Margate Tourism: PO Box 1253, Margate, 4275, tel. (039) 312-2332, fax (039) 312-1886, e-mail: tmargate@iafrica.com

Scottburgh Tourism: PO Box 82, Scottburgh, 4180, tel. (039) 976-1364, fax (039) 978-3114, e-mail: publicity@scottburgh.co.za

Umtamvuna Publicity: PO Box 235, Port Edward, 4295, tel. (039) 313-2026, fax (039) 313-2032, e-mail: hibhome@iafrica.com

Wild Coast Casino: PO Box 23, Port Edward, 4295, tel. (039) 305-9111. For reservations: (011) 780-7800

Zululand
& The Battlefields

LEFT *Kudu graze peacefully in the Ithala Game Reserve, one of KwaZulu-Natal's premier game reserves* (see *page 112*).

ABOVE *A Zulu man wearing his traditional attire sits outside a homestead at Shaka's Kraal, one of the 'living museums' in Zululand.*

ZULULAND & THE BATTLEFIELDS

The Battlefields · Zulu Historical and Cultural Sites · Game Reserves

The rolling hills, grasslands and historic towns of northern KwaZulu-Natal – an area that is generally known as 'the Battlefields' – echo with the heroic and often tragic deeds of the past. The battles between the Boers, British and Zulus that were fought in these hills and valleys some 120 years ago changed the course of South African history. On paper these battles may sound thrilling, but today many of the sites are little more than open grasslands dotted with sad memorials.

Unless you have some understanding of the historical significance of the area, a good place to start would be on a guided tour that will give context to your visit. You can also drive yourself to each site, or tour some of them on horseback, which invokes a wonderfully authentic feel.

Sites of cultural significance to the Zulu nation abound in what is generally referred to as Zululand – the part of the province north of the Tugela River, excluding Maputaland (*see* page 118). But the apartheid government of the past did not consider these sites to be of any interest or importance, and, still today, some are little more than a small plaque on a tree in a remote valley.

However, in recent years, the graves of the Zulu kings, important members of the royal Zulu household and the great royal Zulu homesteads, which were razed to the ground by the British imperial forces, are now being restored, developed and made more accessible by the KwaZulu Monuments Council and Heritage Trust.

No culture is static, especially in Africa where traditional life is constantly under threat of modernisation. Despite this, many cultural practices remain intact in rural Zululand. However, it can be difficult to experience traditional culture first hand. One way to do this, is to visit one of the many cultural villages, or what many people refer to as 'living museums'. Here it is possible to have a glimpse at a life and traditions that are slowly being eroded.

Zululand is also home to some of the country's finest game reserves. Herds of plains game grazing under umbrella acacias, antelope skittering across a dusty pan, hippo honking in the waterways and pans, giraffe silhouetted against the setting sun, and the smell of the African bush in the early hours of the morning are the very epitome of Zululand, drawing visitors from all over the world.

ABOVE *The sphinx-like Isandlwana hill is the site of one of Britain's worst defeats by the Zulu during the Anglo-Zulu War of 1879.*

OPPOSITE TOP *The sad monument to the Boers who beat the British during the Battle of Spioenkop, which took place in 1900.*

OPPOSITE BOTTOM *The Spioenkop Nature Reserve near Lady-smith in the northern KwaZulu-Natal bushveld is home to a variety of game animals, including white rhino, giraffe and zebra. The dam is popular among watersport enthusiasts, and visitors can stay over in chalets or in tents.*

THE BATTLEFIELDS

The political destruction of southern Africa during the Anglo-Zulu and Anglo-Boer wars had repercussions that have lasted into this century. To this day, many relatives and those interested in military history continue to visit the sites of famous battles that rocked the British, weakened the Boers and broke the mighty Zulu nation. Even if you are not interested in the battles of the past, many of these sites are worth a visit. They are beautiful in their own right, and, when the wind blows through the blond grass and the long shadows of evening fall over the lonely gravesites, the haunting loveliness of the African landscape recalls the ghosts of the past. Most of the major

sites are easily accessible, well-qualified guides are available and brochures can be obtained from local tourism offices. There are also smaller sites to be visited that are signposted and not far off the main roads. For instance, north of Ballito towards the Tugela River mouth are Fort Pearson and the Ultimatum Tree which have spectacular views over the wide river. A small interpretative display gives information about local historical events. There are also a number of smaller battle sites that can be visited in and around Ulundi (*see* Ondini, page 100).

Spioenkop

Be prepared to spend at least an hour at this battle site, which is situated midway between Ladysmith and Bergville. There is a self-guided trail that begins and ends at the car park and that takes you to the summit of the hill on which the battle took place. The site has been well preserved and a brochure, which can be obtained at the entrance gate to the Spioenkop Dam

Nature Reserve or at some of the information offices in the area, explains the key events of the battle at strategically selected, marked spots along the trail.

The Battle of Spioenkop took place between 20 and 25 January 1900. It followed a dismal 'Black Week' in December 1899 when the British had been defeated by the Boers at Magersfontein, Stormberg and Colenso, making it imperative that something be done to restore the confidence of the troops. Much has been written about the events that took place during the week of the Spioenkop battle, the first and well-known eyewitness accounts being from the pen of the then war correspondent, later to be British prime minister, Winston Churchill. With all the courage and heroism displayed by the British soldiers, this should have been a battle won by the British. However, much of the blame for their defeat is accorded to the weaknesses and ditherings of the British generals.

Zululand & The Battlefields

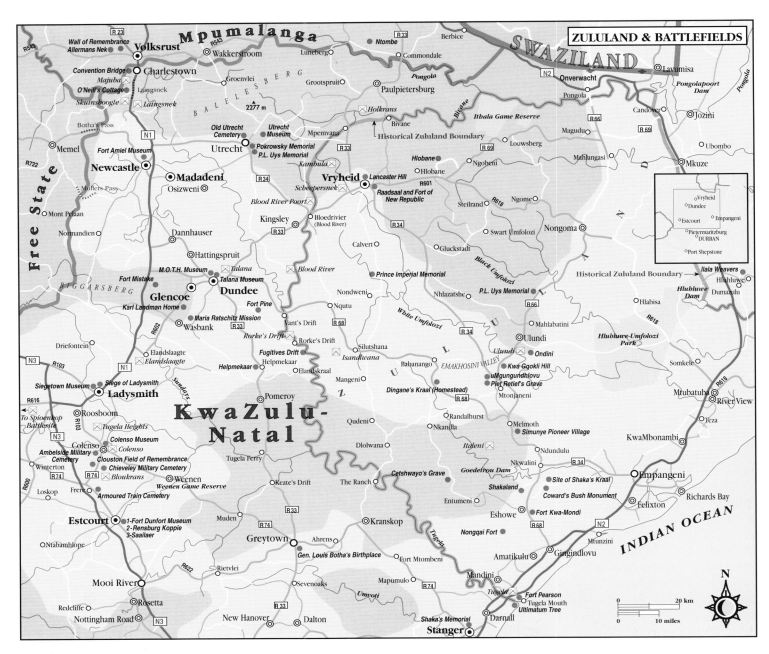

Elandslaagte

The Elandslaagte battlefield is situated just south of the towns of Glencoe and Dundee, and west of Rorke's Drift and Isandlwana. From the parking area at the base of the hills you can see the memorials to the Boers and the Dutch volunteers. This important battle took place on 18 October 1899 and began when General Kock moved his Boer commando towards Elandslaagte to cut off the British troops who were advancing along the Helpmekaar road from Dundee. The British guns were inferior to those of the Boers, and reinforcements were called for. By 16h00 that afternoon the battle had begun. The British charged the hill on which the Boers were entrenched, causing the Boers to retire. The British Imperial Light Horse then charged the retiring Boers, and finally won the day. On your right, on the way to the battlefield, you pass a cemetery under trees. This is the naval cemetery containing graves of some of the soldiers who died during the Battle of Elandslaagte as well as the remains of men who died at Modder River, Sunday's River and Wasbank. Many of these men died from various diseases between March and May 1900 while the British army were camped awaiting the order to advance towards the Biggarsberg.

On the hill opposite the Boer memorial, there is an obelisk to British Lieutenant Colonel Scott-Chrisholme and the Imperial Light Horse, and slightly further along the road is a cemetery containing the graves of more British soldiers who died during the Elandslaagte battle.

Rorke's Drift and Isandlwana

The battles of Rorke's Drift and Isandlwana are perhaps two of the most famous in the area's history. Even if you know little of or have scant interest in past battles, at certain times of the day a sad feeling hangs over these sites, times when you can imagine the aftermath of the ferocious fighting that occurred in these places over 120 years ago.

More than 1 700 British soldiers were killed in January 1879, in what was a furious 2-hour battle when Zulu forces, armed mainly with traditional spears and shields, surprised the British at their camp at the foot of Isandlwana, a strange-looking, sphinx-like mountain. This defeat at the hands of King Cetshwayo's army was a terrible shock to the colonial and British governments in the worst defeat of the era. On the same day, about 4 000 Zulu warriors attacked the small settlement at Rorke's Drift, only to be repulsed by a mere 100-odd British soldiers. Eleven Victoria Crosses were awarded to those who defended Rorke's Drift.

OPPOSITE *There are many lonely graveyards dotted around the historic battlefields, such as this one marking the site of the Anglo-Boer War Battle of Elandslaagte.*

TOP *The Battle of Elandslaagte is also remembered by this solitary stone monument.*

RIGHT *The museum at Rorke's Drift tells the story of the British soldiers who so valiantly defended the small Rorke's Drift settlement following the crushing defeat at Isandlwana.*

95

For an experience of a lifetime, go on a tour with David Rattray of **Fugitives Drift Lodge,** one of the premier guides to these two sites. The battlefields have been Dave's lifelong passion, and visitors, men and women alike, seldom return from a tour with dry eyes. He provides a fully comprehensive experience, beginning over breakfast or dinner at his beautifully situated lodge. Nearby, on a lonely hillside, are the graves of the two men, lieutenants Coghill and Melville, responsible for saving the Queen's colour at the Battle of Isandlwana.

Isandlwana Lodge is also a good place at which to base yourself when touring the battlefields. It is set dramatically on top of the iNyoni Rock formations from where the Zulu commanders directed the battle, and from where you can enjoy unparalleled views of the battlefield. One of the extraordinary features of this lodge is the massive wooden pillars built into the structure, each bearing the name of a great Zulu general.

At Rorke's Drift there is a small but extensive **museum,** as well as a self-guided trail. The original thatched mission house, which was used as a hospital at the time of the battle, has been rebuilt and forms part of the Evangelical Lutheran Mission. The Rorke's Drift ELM **Arts and Crafts Centre,** started by the mission, has become well known. Here you can buy a variety of locally made crafts such as ceramics, painted fabrics and weaving.

Talana Museum and the Miner's Rest Restaurant

The Battle of Talana was the opening battle of the Anglo-Boer War in which the British were victorious. Today, one of the country's most impressive museums, the Talana Museum, stands on this site on the outskirts of Dundee. It comprises nine separate buildings with fascinating exhibits covering the early San hunter-gatherers through to the rise of the Zulu nation and the Anglo-Boer War, as well as the extermination of the cannibals in the early 1900s, who lived in the nearby Biggarsberg. Two buildings that were used by the British as dressing rooms during the Battle of Talana also form part of the museum. A restored miner's cottage close by has been transformed into a pleasant **restaurant** where you can rest and get something to eat.

Blood River Monument

The 64 bronze ox-wagons marking the Blood River battle site, between Dundee and Vryheid, are arranged in the precise laager formation used by the Voortrekkers in 1838 when the massed Zulu impis (battalion of warriors) of King Dingane, numbering about 15 000, advanced on the Boer encampment, only to be slaughtered in their thousands.

The battle at Blood River followed an incident at King Dingane's capital, uMgungundlovu (*see* page 101), when the Voortrekker leader Piet Retief and some 100 members of his group were butchered by warriors. Following these gruesome killings, the Voortrekkers made a covenant with God that, should he grant them victory, they would build a church in his honour (*see* page 50, Voortrekker Museum), and, forever after, observe the date as a day of thanksgiving. Today, 16 December is still a public holiday in South Africa, known as the Day of Reconciliation.

Maria Ratschitz Mission

While you are visiting the battle sites in the area, it would be worth your while to make a detour to the Maria Ratschitz Mission. Established in 1889 by two Trappist monks, the mission has a wonderfully rich, although somewhat sad, history, and it has seen some difficult and traumatic times. The mission farm is owned by the Catholic Church and lies in a beautiful rural setting at the base of the Hlatikulu Mountain near the small town of Wasbank.

The mission was once a vibrant and active centre that fell into disrepair when the community it

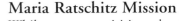

LEFT *The 64 bronze ox-wagons that mark the site of the Battle of Blood River, when a massed Zulu* impi *was defeated by the Boers in 1838.*

had served for many years was badly affected by the apartheid laws introduced in the country. It initially survived the turbulent introduction of the 1913 Land Act, the basis of separating blacks and whites in South Africa, but the forced removals in the late 1960s and early 1970s saw many hundreds of people who had been connected to the mission leave the area. After 1975, without a viable community to serve, there was no longer a resident priest and the mission stagnated and fell into decline.

After the political changes of 1991, it was possible to look at redeveloping this mission, which had once played such a significant role in the community. Today, the cathedral has been restored and its buildings are being returned to their former glory. The spire of the beautiful church can be seen for miles around, and the bells, which are rung three times a day, can again be heard throughout the valley.

Services are held every Sunday and it is worthwhile visiting the mission to attend one of the religious festivities, particularly at Easter or Christmas.

ZULU HISTORICAL AND CULTURAL SITES

The name 'KwaZulu-Natal' gives some indication of the history of this province; 'Natal' referring to the name given by the early white explorers when they sailed close to the coastline on Christmas day in the 1400s, and 'KwaZulu' meaning the place of the Zulu. While there is much to see in the province, it would be unfortunate if you missed the opportunity to visit some of the places where you can learn about the traditions, history and culture of the Zulu people. The Zulu are an integral part of not just the province, but of the whole of southern Africa, and their history is inextricably linked to the development of the entire region.

eMakhosini and Surrounds

The eMakhosini – a remote valley between Ulundi and Babanango – is of great significance to the Zulu nation. The history of the eMakhosini, or Valley of the Kings, dates back to the Stone Age, when early hunter-gatherers resided in the hills and valleys. Throughout the area there is also evidence of the San people, of later Iron Age farmers and of the fifteenth-century settlements associated with the Buthelezi and Khumalo clans – people who later played a significant role in the formation of the Zulu Kingdom.

In about 1785, the great Zulu warrior King Shaka was born in the eMakhosini, and it is also here that his forebearers, amaKhosi Zulu, Phunga, Mageba, Ndaba, Jama, Senzan-gakhona and Dinizulu lie buried. Many of the sites of the older graves have not yet been restored or been developed as tourist attractions, but steps are being taken to purchase land and to preserve the Zulu history and culture, which have left an indelible mark on South Africa.

Even though the sites are sometimes a little difficult to find, they are rewarding to visit. On misty evenings or crisp early

The Reed Dance

In September every year, the reed dance (*umhlanga*) is held at Enyokeni in Zululand. It is a dance of the virgins, at which, according to tradition, the king would choose one of the maidens to become his newest wife. For many years, this ceremony was not performed in Zululand, although it has always been a big affair in the neighbouring kingdom of Swaziland. However, for a number of reasons, some related to the increase in teenage pregnancies being experienced in rural parts of the country, the ceremony has once again been revived to promote chastity and is now a big event on the Zululand cultural calendar. It is one of the most interesting and spectacular ceremonies to observe, where hundreds of bare-breasted young women, adorned with wonderfully colourful beadwork and carrying long canes, swing and sing in rows before the assembled audience. If you are interested in witnessing this spectacular event, it is advisable to contact Tourism KwaZulu-Natal (*see* page 117) to arrange a guide.

Young Zulu maidens dressed in their traditional costumes and carrying reeds prepare to participate in the revived umhlanga, *or reed dance.*

mornings, the atmosphere at some of these lonely graves evokes the spirit of ancient Africa. Until the sites have been properly developed and signposted, it is advisable first to contact the KwaZulu Monuments Council or Melmoth Tourism (*see* page 117) to help you find them or to provide you with a guide.

Other sites of historical importance that you will find in the eMakhosini Valley area as well as south of Ulundi include the **Ulundi Battle Monument,** which marks the site of the last battle of the Anglo-Zulu War of July 1879. At **Nodwengu** a site museum has been erected next to the grave of King Mpande, which lies in the centre of Ulundi. Nodwengu was the Zulu capital during Mpande's rule.

KwaGqokli Hill, the site of Shaka's first military success against the powerful Ndwandwe people in 1818, can be seen from a lay-by on the R66 between Melmoth and Vryheid (take the Ulundi turn-off – a small plaque at the lay-by on the right-hand side of the road tells the story of the battle).

The **grave of Piet Retief,** the Voortrekker leader who, along with many of his compatriots, was clubbed to death and impaled on the orders of Dingane while visiting him in his homestead, can also be visited just north of Melmoth on the Vryheid road.

Fort Nolela is where the British under Lord Chelmsford camped before crossing the river to engage the Zulu in the final battle of Anglo-Zulu War.

About 30 kilometres from Eshowe along the gravel road to Empangeni is a monument that marks the site of **Kwa-Bulawayo,** Shaka's first homestead in about 1816.

On the main road from Melmoth to Vryheid, you can see Dingane's personal water source, the **Mthonjaneni** (meaning 'place of the little spring'), now a national monument, along with a nearby British army fort.

Ondini

Just south of present-day Ulundi, you will find Ondini (meaning 'high place'), once the military capital of King Cetshwayo who became king of the Zulus in 1873. The entire capital was destroyed by fire in 1879 following the Zulu defeat by the British

in the Battle of Ondini. The British had orchestrated a conflict with the powerful but relatively peaceful Zulu nation that lay on their borders. This conflict led to the Anglo-Zulu War in 1879.

The Ondini site consists of an interpretative centre with a **museum,** a statue of King Cetshwayo and a partial reconstruction of the great homestead. Someone is always available to take you around the tiny museum which houses a magnificent bead-work collection, exhibits of various sub-cultures of the Zulu people and a contemporary Zulu children's arts and crafts exhibition. An interesting exhibit explains the rites of passage, or 'life cycle', of the Zulu in their society, from birth to death. Another exhibit portrays their culture in transition. A huge silver mug, presented to King Cetswayo by Queen Victoria, went missing for many years and has only recently been relocated and placed in the museum. An original, poignant letter written by a British soldier to his family, the day after the Battle of Ondini, is also on display.

The massive military complex is in the process of being reconstructed for tourism. As you wander around the field, you will come across a large rock upon which Cetshwayo used to sit when he was being bathed, and from where he could see out across the hills.

It is a Zulu tradition that the re-use of royal land is restricted, so, until recently when reconstruction of the Ondini site began, it had not been significantly touched since its destruction in 1879. Across the way from the homestead is a reconstruction of a **traditional Zulu homestead,** where visitors can stay over-night. Grazing nearby is a herd of white Nguni cattle, much like those so highly prized by the warrior kings of old.

PREVIOUS PAGES *In the Eshowe district in Zululand* imizi, *or homesteads, nestle close to the river from which the people draw their water.*

TOP *The grave of the revered Voortrekker leader Piet Retief keeps a vigil on a lonely hill in Zululand north of Melmoth.*

LEFT *In a secluded and shady spot tucked into the side of a hill, a plaque marks the once important site of King Dingane's personal water source.*

OPPOSITE TOP *Stone stairs wind up the mountainside to the African fantasy bedrooms at Simunye Pioneer Village, a cross-cultural bush lodge near Eshowe.*

OPPOSITE BOTTOM *Like an eagle's nest high on the cliff face, the rooms at Simunye have spectacular views of the river and valley below.*

uMgungundlovu

Situated south of Ulundi, uMgungundlovu was the royal capital of Zululand during the reign of King Dingane and one of many military complexes that he established throughout Zululand. Dingane was instrumental in the murder of his half-brother, Shaka, and succeeded him as king of the Zulu. The name uMgungundlovu roughly translates into 'the secret conclave of the elephant' or 'the place of the elephant'. The word *indlovu* is a metaphorical reference to the stature of the king.

Today, the entire site – where visitors are free to wander around – is of great historical importance and is under archaeological research. So far, the charcoal remains of the outer palisade, which enclosed a massive kraal housing up to 7 000 residents, have been uncovered by archaeologists, allowing a section of the royal area to be reconstructed. Further excavations have exposed a number of the original dwelling floors that were baked hard like pottery when Dingane ordered uMgungundlovu to be burnt down in 1838 after their defeat at the Battle of Blood River (*see* page 96) and in anticipation of the approaching Boers forces. However, one of the most exciting archaeological finds has been the floor of the king's home. It has a diameter of approximately 10 metres, probably the largest house ever to be built in the traditional Zulu manner. The written records of whites who visited the royal homestead of Dingane mention that the king's house was built with no less than 22 supporting posts. Charcoal remains of these posts have been found, as well as the unique six-pointed hearth that is not found in any other Zulu homes, verifying that this was indeed Dingane's home.

Excavations of a copper smithing site, grain pits and other areas of importance can also be seen. As the site is developed for tourism, there are plans to re-erect some of the other permanent structures and conserve the area as authentically as possible. Sometimes a guide is available to take you around the kraal, but, if not, a very informative leaflet will give you all the background you need.

Simunye Pioneer Village

Simunye Pioneer Village near Melmoth offers much the same programme as Shakaland (*see* page 102), only the venue is smaller and more intimate, making it feel more authentic than Shakaland, and its spectacular setting and accommodation evokes an African fantasy. One of the highlights of a visit to Simunye is a ride into the valley. Vehicles are left at a safe car park on a hill, and guests cover the short distance to the village either on horseback or by ox-wagon. On arrival, a Zulu impi bearing flaming torches meets you at the entrance to the village. As there is no electricity, light is provided by hurricane lamps or candles. But this does not mean that Simunye is by any means rustic. It is an up-market venue to rival any of the bigger places.

If there are any traditional celebrations happening in the area outside the village, you may be lucky enough to be taken to see 'the real thing'. Most of the people working at Simunye are connected to the Biyele clan, who have been closely associated with Zulu royalty since the times of the great Zulu warrior kings. The elders of the Biyela lineage are also perhaps one of the last repositories of Zulu oral history, and some of Simunye's staff are the grandchildren, great-grandchildren or at least relatives of famous Zulu generals and warriors who fought in the Anglo-Zulu wars.

Shakaland

In the Nkwalini Valley south of Melmoth lies Shakaland, originally built as the set for the internationally acclaimed film, Shaka Zulu, and perhaps one of the better known cultural villages in Zululand. It has been converted into a traditional Zulu homestead with thatched beehive houses arranged in a circle around the central cattle kraal, and, while the accommodation is also in beehive houses, all the modern conveniences have been added. Guests can join tours – run twice a day – which start with an explanation of the lay-out of a traditional Zulu homestead. After officially entering the homestead, you can wander around the homes and watch women doing beadwork and making traditional pottery, and there is usually an opportunity for you to taste traditional Zulu beer.

ABOVE *A Zulu chief acts out the old traditions of the Zulu nation outside a beehive hut at Shakaland, a well-known cultural village near Melmoth.*

LEFT *As the sun sets, guests at Shakaland gather at the bar for a sundowner before enjoying a traditional Zulu meal.*

OPPOSITE TOP *When making beer in the traditional way, the liquid is separated from the husks using a hand-woven grass strainer.*

OPPOSITE BOTTOM *Dressed in their traditional attire, this group of young Zulus relaxes in the sun at Shakaland.*

You can also witness the age-old methods of making spears and shields, skills that are, to a large extent, disappearing. At Shakaland lives one of the few men who still know how to make the broad stabbing spear introduced by King Shaka. A memorable part of the tour is the demonstration of spear throwing, which visitors are given an opportunity to try themselves if they wish, as well as the stick-fighting demonstrations and a visit to a *sangoma* (or traditional healer).

But, without a doubt, the highlight is the foot-stomping, ground-shaking demonstrations of traditional dance.

Zululand & The Battlefields

Dumazulu Kraal

Dumazulu is conveniently situated near Hluhluwe village, close to the Hluhluwe-Umfolozi Park, the Greater St Lucia Wetlands Park and Mkuze Game Reserve. It was officially opened by King Goodwill Zwelethini, the current Zulu King who is a descendent of King Shaka Zulu. The staff at Dumazulu have tried to maintain the authenticity of the customs and traditions practised during the days of the great warrior king.

Graham Stewart is a world-renowned anthropologist, who, together with his team, conducts daily tours around the village explaining many of the fascinating aspects of Zulu life. Tours include a traditional lunch consisting of, among other things, braaied meat, pumpkin, pap and beans. A walk around the village takes about an hour and a half, ending in a spectacular display of Zulu dancing, and it is not surprising that the place is called Dumazulu, meaning 'thundering Zulu'. Displays of beadmaking, basketry, woodcarving, spearmaking and pottery-making are all part of the experience. There is even an opportunity to taste some traditional Zulu beer and to visit a *sangoma* (traditional healer), for a bone-throwing session.

A stay overnight can also provide an exciting cultural experience. The units are arranged in two circular formations in keeping with the traditional style of architecture, and each representing a different southern African ethnic group.

But your experience does not end there. Adjacent to the village is a snake and crocodile park. Of particular interest is a 350-kilogram, 4-meter-long crocodile, one of the largest in captivity. Demonstrations are given daily.

OPPOSITE *On her head a young Zulu woman at Dumazulu cultural village near Hluhluwe carries an intricately woven waterproof basket, typically associated with women from the Hlabisa district.*

ABOVE *At Dumazulu visitors get the opportunity to watch Zulu women practising their age-old beadwork craft.*

BELOW *Zulu dancers at Dumazulu recreate their colourful and dramatic traditional dances for tourists* (LEFT); *a Zulu warrior dressed in traditional costume sits in front of a grass mat on which are laid out roots and bark used by traditional healers* (RIGHT).

Craft Markets

Many of the craft markets seen alongside the road on the way to some of the game reserves have been initiated with the support and assistance of the KwaZulu-Natal Conservation Service's Neighbour Relations Programme (*see* page 115). The programme has been working primarily with women, aiming to develop not only their craft-making skills, but, in some cases, also their business skills. Some of these projects have greatly empowered the impoverished rural Zulu women living near game reserves, many of whom are the sole breadwinners of large families. At the same time, the projects support and encourage the use of traditional skills.

Although most of the products sold at any of the rural craft centres are made by the people themselves or are obtained locally, items from other areas – or even other African countries – can often also be purchased. Each area has a speciality or craft for which it is well known, for instance, **Mdletsheni Curios** at Hluhluwe-Umfolozi Park's Memorial Gate specialises in beadwork; at the craft market at the **Mambeni Gate** entrance to the Hluhluwe-Umfolozi Park, you can buy fine embroidery and magnificent *amaQutha* – beer baskets for which the women from the nearby Hlabisa district have become world famous. At the entrance to **Sodwana Bay** (*see* page 130) you can buy, among other things, beautifully coloured Zulu baskets, while the **St Lucia** (*see* page 120) area is renowned for Zulu beadwork and decorative mats, and at Mkuzi's **KwaJobe Village** (*see* page 128), you can buy wooden platters and baskets. The craft centre outside **Weenen Game Reserve** (*see* page 117) is well known for its clay pots, and, at **Wagendrift,** you can buy traditional attire and wooden platters. At the **Drakensberg resorts** (*see* pages 68–77), such as Cathedral Peak and Giant's Castle, excellent basketwork is available, as well as at the Royal Natal National Park, where good beadwork can also be bought.

As there are no 'middle men' at these centres, profits go directly into the pockets of the individual artists and crafters, many of whom are support up to 15 people on their income. By supporting the centres, not only can you obtain some exquisite traditional Zulu arts and crafts at competitive prices, but you are also contributing directly to these previously disadvantaged communities.

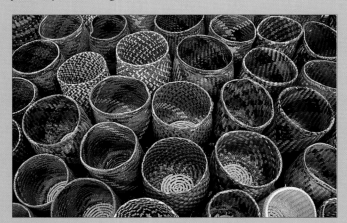

Traditional crafts such as baskets, beadwork, woodcarvings and pottery are sold along KwaZulu-Natal's roadsides.

Songs of Zululand

A unique and innovative project, Songs of Zululand is undertaken by schools in the Mtubatuba-Hluhluwe region to give visitors an opportunity to meet young rural South Africans and to listen to their wonderful music, while at the same time giving these youngsters from fairly isolated communities the chance not only to perform for an audience but also to interact with outsiders, as well as to raise money for their often impoverished schools.

Each day of the week (Mondays to Fridays) students from a different school along the road between the **Hluhluwe-Umfolozi Park** and the town of **Mtubatuba** perform the songs and dances of Zululand for tourists – and anyone else who may be interested. The project began in response to a request by schoolchildren in these rural districts to meet tourists. The schools are all well signposted, and it is simply a matter of driving off the main road between the entrance to the reserve and Mtubatuba and a short way into rural Zululand in order to participate in the dance performances.

On arrival, visitors are met by the teachers and it is interesting to discover how they feel about living and teaching in rural areas, often without electricity or any of the basic resources so often taken for granted in urban centres. The students perform adaptations of traditional songs and dances that would once have told of great Zulu warriors or their preparations for battle. Nowadays, the variations of those songs tend to reflect the transitions that the culture of these young people is undergoing.

The songs, often about studying for exams and going to the city to find work, and dances are not composed or choreographed for tourists, but are the actual songs and dances that these children use in rituals in their daily lives – such as at church services, weddings, and other celebrations and festivities.

Dances that are performed include *Isicathamiya* (a slow song and dance form performed without the accompaniment of any musical instruments), Afro-gospel, *Imbohohlo* (wedding songs), *Izinyoni Ezimhlope* (a more modern music form fusing old with new), *Ingoma* (performed by boys and girls together), gumboot dancing (a modern form of *Ingoma*, which developed on the Durban docks and was transported to the mines), and *Indlamu* (a traditional dance most commonly associated with Zulu culture with drums and full traditional attire). In each case an explanation is given of why and when these routines are used in real life. There is ample opportunity for visitors to chat to the students after the performance, if they wish to find out more about the Zulu way of life.

Although there is no charge for the shows, donations are encouraged. Do not give any money directly to the children, though, as the money is administered by the **Mtubatuba Publicity Association** and goes towards school projects. In this way, both the tourists and the students, and therefore the community at large, benefit.

The Ilala Weavers shop in Hluhluwe village is packed with craftwork of immense skill and beauty, and there is always someone on hand to give you an explanation of what the items are, and, if it is a traditional item, how it would be used in a Zulu home. The items are sometimes a little more pricey here than elsewhere, but the quality is outstanding. Attached to the shop is a lovely restaurant overlooking a garden with big, shady trees.

KwaDukuza

Very few people visiting South Africa do not know of King Shaka, the man who is credited with building the Zulu people into a mighty warrior nation. KwaDukuza, where the modern-day town of Stanger stands, was the site of Shaka's last great capital. An old mahogany tree grows in front of the municipal offices and it was here, according to legend, that Shaka was assassinated by his two half-brothers, Dingane and Mhlangane. Nearby is an interpretative centre with more information about the great warrior king.

Other local sites of cultural interest are **Shaka's Spring**, from where, at the time of Shaka's residence, unpolluted water was fetched for the king. Shaka's swimming and bathing place on the Imbozamo River, **Shaka's Cave**, a shelf above the bathing place where King Shaka would rest, and **The Execution Cliff**, where ordered executions took place, are other places of interest.

Ilala Weavers

When Ilala Weavers was established some 20 years ago, traditional Zulu handicrafts were in danger of dying out. Ilala Weavers has helped, and continues to help, rural Zulu people to use their skills, thereby attaining some level of self-sufficiency. The people all work from home, bringing their products to Ilala Weavers where it is marketed, both locally and internationally. As well as continuing to make many traditional items, the people have also learned to craft more modern products, such as woven lampshades, salad servers, key-rings, pencil dolls and a wide range of fashion accessories. In an adaptation of the traditional grass *menge* – a small saucer-shaped bowl used to cover clay beer pots – brightly coloured telephone wire is now used instead of grass, and the end products are striking in both colour and pattern.

ABOVE *Many of the traditional Zulu crafts such as basket-weaving are still learned and practised in rural areas. The basket-makers of Ilala Weavers, a traditional handicraft shop in Hluhluwe, work from home and bring their finished products to the shop to be sold.*

RIGHT *Roadside shops in rural areas, such as this one in Hluhluwe village, are often brightly decorated in simulations of ethnic African design.*

GAME RESERVES

Most of the game reserves in northern KwaZulu-Natal and Zululand are run by the Kwa-Zulu-Natal Nature Conservation Service, but there are also a number of excellent privately run game reserves, conservancies and biosphere reserves.

Like most of the country's national and provincial game reserves and parks, those run by the KwaZulu-Natal Nature Conservation Service are open to the public, who can tour and view game from the comfort of their own vehicles. The roads are generally good, except, maybe, after some heavy rains have fallen.

Accommodation, both in and outside the reserves, is plentiful and within a wide price range, and the facilities and services offered are generally excellent.

Hluhluwe-Umfolozi Park

Situated about 250 kilometres north of Durban, Hluhluwe-Umfolozi is one of the province's premier reserves and one of the biggest in South Africa – 96 000 hectares. It is a 'big five' reserve, offering black and white rhino, buffalo, lion, leopard and elephant, as well as all the plains animals and including species such as red duiker, which are not always as prolific in other reserves. Animals you could see here, and which do not always occur in reserves elsewhere in KwaZulu-Natal are the elusive cheetah and endangered wild dog. The range and habitat of wild dog have decreased dramatically in Africa, and today they are a seriously threatened species. The park also boasts more than 1 250 different species of plants and trees in a mosaic of biologically diverse habitats.

Hluhluwe and Umfolozi, both founded in 1895, used to be two separate parks and are two of Africa's oldest game reserves, with an atmosphere that you are unlikely to experience elsewhere. In the days of the great Zulu warrior King Shaka, parts of Umfolozi were favoured royal hunting grounds. Later the colonists came to hunt with their guns, driving many species to the brink of extinction before drastic measures were taken to protect the game. In 1989, the 'corridor area' between the two parks was incorporated, and today this area is also managed as part of the reserve.

OPPOSITE TOP *There is great excitement when a cheetah cub is sighted at the Hluhluwe-Umfolozi Park.*

OPPOSITE BOTTOM *The distinctive and unique white ring on the rump of this antelope identifies it as a waterbuck, seen here at the Hluhluwe-Umfolozi Park.*

ABOVE *Rare black rhino can be seen at a number of the province's game reserves, thanks to the conservation effort known as Operation Rhino, which was largely responsible for saving the rhino from near extinction.*

Operation Rhino

The story of rhino is the story of Hluhluwe-Umfolozi, the place where Operation Rhino was launched in the early 1960s. The recovery of the white rhino from near extinction is one of the great success stories of African wildlife conservation as poaching and hunting had decimated Africa's rhino population, both black and white. The aim of Operation Rhino was to transport surplus numbers of white rhino from Hluhluwe-Umfolozi to other protected areas, and, by the end of 1996, the number of rhino relocated world-wide had reached a total of more than 8 000, approximately 7 000 of which had been resettled in other protected areas within South Africa. This unprecedented conservation effort saw rhino return from the brink of extinction, and today it is safe to say that these two reserves remain the 'bread-basket' of both black and white rhino in Africa. At present, there are an estimated 1 475 rhino on private land in the country.

The Natal Parks Board (forerunner of the KwaZulu-Natal Nature Conservation Service) set up their now internationally acclaimed Game Capture Unit in the mid-1960s and to date it has caught more than 123 000 animals of 34 species. Some are sold on auction to private game farms, some are moved to other reserves and some are donated to other conservation areas throughout Africa.

In the corridor area of the park, the terrain flattens out, becoming more open. In other areas of the park, though, the habitats range from savanna and grassland to forest and woodland. In the north are deep valleys and ravines, rivers and forests, and in early summer the hillsides are covered in the soft purple haze of flowering Cape chestnut trees. The evocative Black and White Mfolozi rivers, settings for many game ranger tales, wind through the Umfolozi section of the park, while the Hluhluwe and Manzimbomvu rivers cut through the Hluhluwe section.

Apart from the drives you can undertake in your own vehicle, the park offers self-guided foot trails, as well as day walks, game drives and wilderness trails led by experienced staff. As there are no roads on the wilderness trails and access is only by foot, disturbance by humans is kept to a minimum. The **Traditional**

ABOVE *The beautifully situated chalets at Hilltop Camp in the Hluhluwe reserve look out over the unspoilt bush.*

CENTRE *Vultures cluster around a carcass in the Hluhluwe reserve.*

LEFT *Rocky outcrops in the Hluhluwe reserve provide ideal roosting sites for the bald ibis.*

OPPOSITE TOP *The bad-tempered and often dangerous buffalo is one of the Hluhluwe-Umfolozi Park's 'big five', along with rhino, elephant, lion and leopard.*

OPPOSITE BOTTOM *Hiking through the Umfolozi reserve with a ranger who knows the habits of the animals is very rewarding.*

Wilderness Trail starts and ends at Mndindini Tented Camp and is a four-night trail, and there is also a **Weekend Wilderness Trail** and the Bushveld Trails. The **Bushveld Trails** are only run from December to March, enabling hikers to enjoy the wilderness during the heat of the summer months. Hikers are driven to and from the camp on the edge of the wilderness area where they can enjoy excellent game-viewing, and early-morning and late-afternoon walks are organised into the wilderness area, making use of the coolest parts of the day. Umfolozi's **Primitive Trail** caters for enthusiasts who wish to combine backpacking and sleeping under the stars. Hikers carry their own kit and are accompanied by a trail guide. A campfire burns all night to keep the wild animals at bay, and each person sits a 90-minute watch. The park also offers a **Wilderness Canoe Safari** in the summer months when the rivers are fuller.

Lodges, camps, bush lodges and bush camps are available to suit all tastes and budgets, many offering the services of a cook. **Mpila**, perched high on a hill overlooking the wilderness area of Umfolozi, has a thatched rest camp with communal ablution blocks and self-contained cottages. Mpila's **Safari Tented Camp** nestles on the side of the hill. Mpila is reached from the northeast via the Mtubatuba/Nongoma road through the Nayalzi Gate entrance, or from the west via the Ulundi road through Cengweni Gate.

Another small camp at Umfolozi is **Masinda,** and there is also the more luxurious **Masinda Lodge.** On the banks of the Black Mfolozi River are situated the **Sontuli, Nselweni** and **Mndin-**dini bush camps, and, although these camps are out in the wild, they are comfortable and also have cooks in attendance.

In the Hluhluwe section of the park lies **Hilltop Camp.** This is one of the KwaZulu-Natal Nature Conservation Service's largest developments and is situated right on the edge of a steep forested slope, with breathtaking views of Zululand's hills and valleys stretching out before you. Although many of the chalets are self-catering, meals can be enjoyed at the Mpunayne Restaurant.

Close to Hilltop Camp lies **Mtwazi Lodge,** and hidden in the wilderness setting overlooking the Hluhluwe River is **Muntulu Bush Lodge,** which affords guests total privacy and an amazing wildlife experience. Hluhluwe's other bush lodges are **Gqoyeni, Munyawaneni** and **Hlathikhulu.**

Ithala Game Reserve

Ithala is perhaps one of the most underrated of the province's reserves, as more people tend to visit the bigger and better-known ones such as the Hluhluwe-Umfolozi Park. For some people, however, the less busy a place is, the more attractive they find it. Much of the Ithala reserve was once agricultural land that has been rehabilitated and largely restored to its former natural state. Scenically, Ithala rates as one of the most beautiful and interesting reserves, experiencing great seasonal contrasts. Situated in the north of KwaZulu-Natal, close to the border with Swaziland, it overlooks the Pongola River valley and consists predominantly of rugged, mountainous thornveld, with areas of open grassland.

Ithala carries elephant, black and white rhino, giraffe, buffalo and a wide variety of other game such as zebra, giraffe and warthog. Not often seen are leopard and hyena, although you will sometimes hear hyena cackling in the night. As there are no lion, the game are more relaxed, and, perhaps for this reason, viewing seems easier.

Apart from the superb opportunities for game-watching, Ithala is well known for its incredible geological diversity – some of the oldest rock formations in the world are found here, dating back 3 000 million years. This varied topography has given rise to a great diversity of habitats for both plants and animals.

Ithala's main camp, **Ntshondwe**, is magnificently situated against a backdrop of cliffs, from which it takes its name. These

TOP *After a day of game-viewing, a moment can be enjoyed looking out over Ithala's Ntshondwe camp and the vast African landscape.*

OPPOSITE *A giraffe crosses the road right in front of a game-viewing vehicle at Ithala Game Reserve.*

LEFT *The comical warthog with their little tusks and upturned tails are a favourite with visitors, but can be quite dangerous.*

ABOVE *With their distinctive black and white markings, zebra are one of the most striking animals to encounter in the bush.*

dolerite and sandstone cliffs are a haven for raptors that soar high above this cleverly camouflaged camp, which consists of 39 thatched chalets nestling among the wild fig, acacia and cassonia trees.

At the centre of the camp is the visitors' centre and a restaurant overlooking a small pan. There is also a fully equipped conference centre, a bar, a swimming pool and an excellent curio shop where, among a variety of goods, they also sell high-quality locally made crafts, as well as basic provisions.

Ntshondwe's luxurious **Ntshondwe Lodge** has its own small swimming pool, barbecue area and a sundeck from where you can enjoy a cool evening looking down on the vast valley below. A cook is available at the lodge, ensuring a truly luxurious and stress-free stay.

RIGHT *The tsessebe antelope found at Ithala Game Reserve are not common in many other reserves in KwaZulu-Natal.*

BELOW *White rhino have been saved from the brink of extinction and are now often seen in the province's game reserves.*

OPPOSITE *With the rocky outcrop at Ntshondwe Camp as a backdrop, visitors on a game drive at Ithala stop to watch a zebra and rhino mother and calf.*

Ithala also boasts three bush camps. **Mhlangeni Bush Camp,** set high on a rocky outcrop, boasts excellent views from the open-plan lounge and sundeck – and from the showers – and **Mbizo Bush Camp** lies beside a series of gurgling rapids and whirling pools near the confluence of the Mbizo and Ngubu rivers. **Thalu Bush Camp** nestles at the foot of a steep slope on the banks of the Thalu River.

KwaZulu-Natal Nature Conservation Service Community Programme

During South Africa's apartheid years, many black communities were forcibly removed from their rural homes in order for game reserves to be established. Not only were they deprived of their land with little or no compensation, but they were also denied access to natural resources upon which they relied for survival. This caused enormous resentment of the conservation authorities by these communities, leading to an uncomfortably tense relationship which still exists in some areas.

The KwaZulu-Natal Nature Conservation Service (KNCS) began its Neighbour Relations Programme in 1992 in an attempt to rectify and improve its relations with its neighbouring communities. Today, this programme is possibly one of the most advanced of its kind in the country. Local management teams have been established to allow for public response and a partnership approach to local environmental issues. The programme includes an Environmental Awareness System for Youth (a school-based programme), the annual International Coastal Clean-Up, during which some 4 000 volunteers undertake to clean up the entire KwaZulu-Natal coastline, a Linefish Management Awareness Programme,

and the Community-Based Tourism Programme, which supports eco-tourism and conservation developments in rural communities. This has been an important and significant programme that has gone a long way towards improving relations with neighbouring communities.

A similar project is the iNyanga Programme that is building relationships between traditional healers and the KNCS. It includes a number of muthi (traditional medicine using indigenous plants and animals) nurseries.

Since 1998, visitors to KNCS game reserves have been required to pay a community levy when entering certain protected areas. The idea behind the levy is that, in order for conservation areas to thrive, they have to have the support of the people. This includes the many disadvantaged communities who live around these areas. The KNCS recognises the needs of these communities and is committed to their development and upliftment through one of the largest conservation and social responsibility programmes in Africa. The levy is used to assist neighbouring communities with training and the development of their areas. It is a once-off payment per camp, per reserve, and varies from area to area.

The Thukela Biosphere

The unique concept of a biosphere reserve was developed to promote conservation and community upliftment through sustainable utilisation of natural resources and the development of tourism. A number of land-owners in the Weenen district have joined their land to form the 100 000 hectares of valley bushveld, known as the Thukela Biosphere, and to develop private game ranches, lodges and bush camps, promoting the area and encouraging visitors.

One of the projects involved in the biosphere is a cultural one designed to promote land reform, tourism development and, through this, job creation for the local people. The area in which many of these communities live is extremely rugged, making it difficult to reach, which is why they have retained their distinctive culture and rich historical heritage. The project encourages some of the typical Zulu traditions and crafts, such as their intricate beadwork and the making of shields, assegais and ethnic costumes. Traditional Zulu dancing can also be seen.

The **Zingela Safari and River Company** is based on the banks of the Tugela River and runs three-day water rafting trip on the Tugela River, taking you 30 kilometres downstream. They also organise big-game hunting safaris within the biosphere.

Umsuluzi Game Park is a private game farm with a camp nestling on the banks of the Bloukrans River. It offers wilderness walks in the 4 000-hectare reserve where some 25 or so species of game can be seen, and both the birding and fishing is good.

Kaisha Game Ranch comprises some 2 000 hectares of African bushveld banking onto the mighty Tugela River. Night drives, mountain biking, river rafting with qualified guides, fishing, birding, game-viewing, limited hunting and visits to a Zulu cultural village are all on offer. The accommodation is either in a small thatched cottage or a larger stone cottage.

Kusa Kusa Game Lodge has a bamboo and thatch cottage, and offers wilderness walks, guided trails and night game drives,

and Zulu dancing can be organised on request. One of the interesting things about **Isambane Camp**, which is located off the Muden road, is the caves, and a hike through the wilderness takes you to them. Hundreds of years ago people mined iron ore here. *Isambane* is the Zulu name for aardvark or antbear, a gentle nocturnal creature that, along with other wild creatures, inhabits this large game farm in the biosphere.

Together, all these privately owned game farms have substantially extended the amount of land under conservation in the province.

OPPOSITE TOP *Noisy little Cape weavers, so named because of their ingenious method of building nests, are a common sight in KwaZulu-Natal.*

OPPOSITE BOTTOM *Wide open spaces and magnificent vistas characterise the environment of Weenen Game Reserve, which lies north of Pietermaritzburg.*

Weenen Game Reserve lies in the core conservation area of the Thukela Biosphere which ensures that the reserve conforms to international criteria as laid down by UNESCO.

This 6 500-hectare reserve, one of the few formally protected stretches of valley bushveld in the country, is well known for its rhino sightings and carries both the white and the endangered black rhino. Another animal that can be seen here is the rare roan antelope. Birding is also good, with 279 recorded species.

Weenen offers a variety of activities, such as night drives, and guided and self-guided walks, and the well-placed water holes guarantee good game-viewing. Visitors can also drive their own vehicles to see game on the 47 kilometres of road. It is one of the few provincial reserves offering a four-wheel-drive trail, although the four-wheel-drive trails in other parts of the biosphere are far more rugged and perhaps more challenging. A small but enchanting campsite is available for camping or caravanning, and there is also a cottage and a tented camp for hire. Those interested in traditional Zulu crafts can visit the craft centre outside the reserve, which is well known for its clay pots.

USEFUL INFORMATION

A number of registered tour guides are available to take you around the battlefields, a list of which can be obtained from any of the local tourist information offices, or from the Tourist Junction in Durban. Note that bookings for provincial reserve campsites can be made via the officers in charge of the various reserves; bookings for other accommodation must be made through the KwaZulu-Natal Nature Conservation Service head office.

Battlefields Route Information: tel. (036) 352-6253,
e-mail: route@battlefields.org.za
Dumazulu Cultural Village: PO Box 359, Hluhluwe, 3960,
tel (035) 562-2260
Dundee Publicity Association: Victoria Street, Dundee,
tel. (034) 212-2121, fax (034) 212-3856
Fugitives Drift Lodge: Dave Rattray, tel. (034) 642-1843
Hluhluwe Publicity Association: PO Box 399, Hluhluwe 3960,
tel. (035) 562-0353
Hluhluwe-Umfolozi Park: Hilltop Camp (035) 562-0255;
Mpila Camp (035) 562-0287
Ilala Weavers: PO Box 195, Hluhluwe, 3960, tel. (035) 562-0630/1
Isandlwana Lodge: PO Box 30, Isandlwana, 3005, tel. (034) 271-8301, fax (034) 271-8306, e-mail: isand@icon.co.za,
website: www.isandlwana.co.za
Ithala Game Reserve: PO Box 98, Louwsburg, 3150,
tel. (034) 907-5105
KwaZulu Monuments Council and Heritage Trust: PO Box 523, Ulundi, 3838, tel. (035) 870-2050/1/2, fax (035) 870-2054
KwaZulu-Natal Nature Conservation Service: Queen Elizabeth Park, PO Box 1306, Cascades, Pietermaritzburg, 3202, tel. (033) 845-1000, fax (033) 845-1001, e-mail: bookings@rhino.org.za

KwaZulu-Natal Tourism: Tourist Junction, 160 Pine Street, Durban, tel. (031) 304-7144, fax (031) 305-6693, e-mail: tkzn@iafrica.com
Ladysmith Cultural Centre and Museum: PO Box 29, Ladysmith, 3370, tel./fax (036) 637-2992
Maria Ratschitz Mission: PO Box 197, Wasbank, 2920,
tel. (034) 651-1097
Melmoth Tourism: PO Box 11, Melmoth, 3835,
tel. (035) 450-2082
Mtubatuba Publicity Association: PO Box 81, Mtubatuba, 3935,
tel. (035) 550-0781, fax (035) 550-0721
Rorke's Drift Arts and Crafts Centre: PO Rorke's Drift, 3016,
tel. (034) 642-1687
Rorke's Drift Museum: PO Rorke's Drift, 3016, tel. (034) 642-1687
Rorke's View Guest Farm (horseback tours): PO Box 683, Dundee, 3000, tel. (034) 642-1741, fax (034) 642-1654
Shakaland: PO Box 103, Eshowe, 3815, tel. (035) 640-0912,
fax (035) 640-0824
Simunye: Protea Hotels, PO Eshowe, 3815, tel. (035) 460-0912, fax (035) 460-0824. Central reservations: (021) 419-8800,
or toll free 0800-11-9000
Talana Museum: Vryheid Road, Dundee, Private Bag 2024, Dundee, 3000, tel. (034) 212-2654, fax (034) 212-2376
Thukela Biosphere Information Centre: For information on Umsuluzi Game Park, Kaisha Game Ranch, Kusa Kusa Game Lodge, Zingela Safari and River Company, and Isambane Camp, contact:
PO Box 202, Weenen, 3325, tel. (036) 541-1938
Weenen Game Reserve: PO Box 122, Weenen, 3325, tel. (036) 354-1809
Zingela Safari and River Company: PO Box 141, Weenen, 3325, tel./fax (036) 354-1962, e-mail: zingela@futurest.co.za

Zululand & The Battlefields

Maputaland –
Wilderness Wonderland

LEFT *The long, empty beaches of Maputaland stretch from St Lucia northwards to Kosi Bay on the border of Mozambique.*

ABOVE *It is indeed an unusual sight to see a loggerhead turtle preparing her nest for laying eggs during the day. This is predominantly done on still, dark nights (see box on page 131).*

$\mathscr{M}$APUTALAND — WILDERNESS WONDERLAND

Greater St Lucia Wetland Park • Phinda Resource Reserve • Maputaland Marine and Coastal Forest Reserves
Tembe Elephant Reserve • Ndumo Game Reserve

$\mathscr{M}$aputaland, a fascinating area where it is still possible to find the last bastions of some of Africa's older cultural practices, such as the traditional fish drives and traps of the Thonga people, lies in the north-eastern section of KwaZulu-Natal. It is bordered in the far north by Mozambique, in the west it is bound by the Lebombo Mountains, to the east lies the Indian Ocean and, in the south, it ends at Lake St Lucia's estuary. Maputaland lies at the point of transition between subtropical and tropical zones, making it home to an extraordinary profusion of indigenous plants and animals not found in many other parts of the country.

Pristine beaches lining the coast are the ancient breeding grounds of the once endangered leatherback and loggerhead turtles. The glorious coral reefs swarm with an incredible variety of colourful fishes, and the crystal-clear waterways are filled with hippo and crocodile, while fish eagle and palmnut vulture soar overhead. Maputaland is synonymous with wildlife, and it is here that you can still hear the voice of ancient Africa.

The entire coastline, stretching from Mapelane Nature Reserve south of St Lucia to Kosi Bay on the Mozambique border and extending 5 kilometres into the ocean, is divided into two marine reserves protecting the magnificent beaches, aquatic life and coral reefs of the northernmost section of South Africa's coastline. Adjoining this unspoilt coastline is a patchwork of conservation areas protecting the region's vegetated dune forests, lake systems, estuaries, swamps, bushveld and riverine forests.

GREATER ST LUCIA WETLAND PARK

Lake St Lucia, Africa's largest estuarine system and part of the vast Greater St Lucia Wetland Park, is a unique lake that stretches for an expansive 38 000 hectares, offering some of the most diverse wildlife and outdoor experiences in the country, including guided wilderness trails (see page 129). With this vastness of water, it is not surprising that St Lucia is famous for its birdlife – especially the thousands of water birds that gather here. The lake supports an enormous population of crocodile and hippo, and there are also rhino, buffalo, waterbuck, impala, nyala, kudu and a host of other wild animals. This can be attributed to the fact that the park incorporates an amazing diversity of habitats, from the Lebombo Mountain range across the grasslands to the forests, wetlands, mangroves and vegetated dunes, down to the long, white beaches and offshore coral reefs. Migrant whales, dolphins, leatherback and loggerhead turtles and an incredible variety of fish can be seen along the coastline.

ABOVE *White pelicans float atop the still waters of Lake St Lucia. These birds are known to feed in flocks, herding fish into shallow water, then scooping them up in their stretchy pouches.*

OPPOSITE *Water-lilies grace the shallow, tranquil waters of Lake Bhangazi in the Greater St Lucia Wetland Park. The lake is considered a sacred place among local people.*

Incorporated into the Greater St Lucia Wetland Park and marine reserve are **Mapelane, False Bay Park, Cape Vidal, Mkuzi Game Reserve** and **Sodwana Bay Park.** The Wetland Park is recognised internationally as a World Heritage Site, and two sections have been registered as Wetlands of International Significance under the Ramsar Convention. Along the western shores of Lake St Lucia are cliffs rich in marine fossils, indicating that the area was once inhabited by ancient and now long-extinct molluscs, relatives of the clams, delicate nautiluses and molluscs of today. Enormous, 16-centimetre-long fossilised sharks' teeth have also been found here.

Archaeological Sites

Ample evidence, possibly dating from before early Stone Age times, exists of the early inhabitants of Maputaland, but, until recently, not much had been done about preserving sites of archaeological importance. The result is that, although there are sites of great interest, not many are accessible to the public. But, if you would like to visit some of the areas off the beaten track, ask one of the conservation officers from the KwaZulu-Natal Nature Conservation Service or staff from the museums, and they may be able to help you visit places such as the shell middens containing early Stone Age pottery south of the Enkwazini River near St Lucia Bay, or Border Cave in the Lebombo Mountains, one of the oldest caves in the country known to have been inhabited by humans. If you are fortunate enough to go to any of these places, remember that it is a crime to touch or remove any artefacts.

The western shores of Lake St Lucia are rich in fossil deposits.

The busy and over-commercialised resort village of **St Lucia**, which has developed at the mouth of the estuary, should in no way be mistaken as representative of what the area has to offer. At St Lucia Estuary, there are a number of caravan and camping sites, walks and opportunities for mountain biking. On the approach to the village, where the bridge crosses the lake, stop at the craft centre on the left-hand side of the road. From here you can explore this amazing lake on the *Santa Lucia* launch. Guided tours depart daily and last up to 2 hours.

OPPOSITE TOP *Fishing boats line up along the beach at Cape Vidal, ready to be launched. The waters off this stretch of coast provide some of the best game-fishing opportunities along the entire South African coast.*

OPPOSITE CENTRE *The majestic and elegant African fish eagle – known for its distinctive call – finds plenty of food in the rich waters of Lake St Lucia.*

OPPOSITE BOTTOM LEFT *A wide variety of water birds, such as the aptly named African spoonbill, paddle around the shallow waters at Lake St Lucia, looking for food.*

OPPOSITE BOTTOM RIGHT *A leisurely trip on the* Santa Lucia *launch is a wonderful way to explore the lake system and observe crocodiles, hippo and the many bird species that live around the water's edge.*

FOLLOWING PAGES *The massive sand dunes at Cape Vidal shift and change shape with the tides and the wind.*

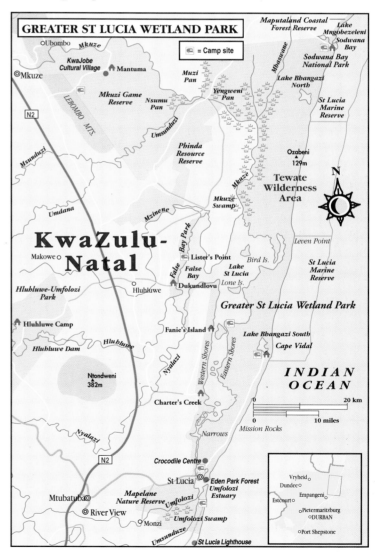

Humming slowly up the lake system on the old double-decker launch is certainly the most rewarding way to see some of the estimated 800 hippo and 1 000 Nile crocodile that inhabit the lake, while enjoying the fantastic diversity of birdlife.

Close to St Lucia village, and at the entrance to the park, is the Crocodile Centre. Tours are conducted, and you will have the opportunity to see baby crocodiles, as well as watch these fascinating reptiles being fed on Saturday afternoons.

TOP LEFT It is not only the fearsome crocodiles that are found in the Greater St Lucia Wetland Park, but also these pretty little tinker reed frogs which inhabit ponds and swamps.

ABOVE Although crocodiles are a common sight in the lakes and rivers around St Lucia, you can see them close up at the Crocodile Centre just outside the village.

CENTRE Enormous, colourful hats are made by Zulu women and sold at the St Lucia estuary craft market.

LEFT A variety of fresh fruit and vegetables is sold on the roadside in the busy resort village of St Lucia.

OPPOSITE TOP The jetty at Fanie's Island is an ideal spot for fishing.

OPPOSITE CENTRE When the heat gets overwhelming, take a refreshing dip in the swimming pool at Charter's Creek, on the shores of Lake St Lucia.

OPPOSITE BOTTOM Charter's Creek is also a favourite destination for seasoned fishermen, who come here to launch their boats on the lake.

Certain areas of the park have been opened up for recreation, and Mission Rocks, 16 kilometres north of St Lucia estuary, has the most wonderful rock pools and a dune-top lookout point from where you can see for miles across the lake, the eastern shores and the sea.

Further up the coast, Cape Vidal's clear blue ocean is popular for sport fishing and snorkelling and it is very busy during holiday periods. The golden beaches and coastal forests are ideal for hiking, and there are a number of self-guided trails that wind through these areas, as well as to the small Lake Bhangazi a little inland.

Situated on the south bank of the Mfolozi River mouth is **Mapelane,** which offers excellent ski-boating, surf-fishing and safe swimming at low tide. On the inland side or western shores

of the lake are places such as **False Bay Park, Fanie's Island** and **Charter's Creek,** all of which are popular fishing spots with excellent rest camps, campsites and other facilities, such as fishing jetties and boat moorings.

In the far north of the park lies **Sodwana Bay Park.** Permits are needed for accessing the beach in a vehicle, and on certain stretches, no privately owned vehicles are allowed (Sodwana Bay is discussed on pages 130–131.)

Maputaland – Wilderness Wonderland

and some 70 black rhino, as well as elephant, leopard, giraffe, cheetah and a variety of other plains game. Prolific herds of zebra, blue wildebeest, impala and nyala can be seen, as well as kudu, eland and the little suni antelope.

The reserve is also world famous for its birds, with 600 species having been spotted here. Six superbly placed hides offer fantastic birding, as well as the chance to watch game coming to the water holes and pans to drink, two of the most beautiful being Nhlonhlela and Nsumo.

The pans are shallow expanses of water, surrounded by a haze of pale lemon-green fever trees (once thought to be the cause of sleeping sickness) and reeds, and in the summer they are lined with water-lilies. Nsumo, the larger of the two pans, has two elevated bird-viewing hides; these provide an amazing vantage point from which to watch a variety of birds, including spurwing geese, and white- and pinkbacked pelicans. African fish eagles can often be spotted swooping down over the pans from their fever-tree perches to snatch their prey from the water. Large populations of hippo and crocodile can be found wallowing in Mkuzi's pans, which also attract a spectacle of aquatic life.

Mkuzi Game Reserve

Just 4 hours' drive from Durban, Mkuzi Game Reserve lies between the Msunduze and Mkuzi rivers at the foot of the Lebombo Moutains in the west. It is approximately 335 kilometres from Durban on the N2, after which you follow the game reserve signs which take you on a gravel road for 16 kilometres, passing through a gorge in the Lebombo range. This 40 000-hectare reserve lies 60 kilometres or so north of the Hluhluwe-Umfolozi Park and forms part of the Greater St Lucia Wetland Park. It also shares a border with the privately owned Phinda Resource Reserve. The Mkuze River, from which the reserve takes its name, flows into a delta that eventually joins the north-eastern tip of magnificent Lake St Lucia.

Situated on the Maputaland coastal plains, Mkuzi Game Reserve is a favourite haunt to which nature lovers return year after year, despite it not being a 'big five' reserve (the big five – elephant, leopard, rhino, buffalo and lion – are the animals that tourists most want to see). Although it is only a fraction of the size of the Kruger National Park in the northeast of the country, Mkuzi supports a population of about 120 white rhino

Guided day and night game drives can be booked at the Mantuma Main Camp office. Many of the animals you encounter during a night drive are seldom seen in the day, and it is thrilling to catch glimpses of the little thick-tailed bush-baby, white-tailed mongoose, porcupine, small spotted genet, hyena and even sometimes leopard. Also look out for nocturnal birds such as owls, dikkops and nightjars.

If you would prefer a more intimate experience of the African bush than driving around in a car, a guided walking trail to look at the game and birds is an option. The **Fig Forest Walk** leads through Mkuzi's spectacular fig forest, taking you into cool glades beneath the dense, green canopy of the giant sycamore trees. The twisted ropes of roots and entwined trunks are home to some beautiful birds, such as narina trogans and purple-crested louries. Trumpeter hornbills wail in the foliage, forest weavers leap and hop, whitebacked vultures and gabar goshawks roost in the upper branches, and, if you are lucky, you may spot the elusive Pel's fishing owl. A longer wilderness trail will take you, on foot, into the bush for three days; you will be accommodated overnight in the tented trails camps (*see* box, this page).

Within the boundaries of Mkuzi Game Reserve lies the **sacred burial site** of chiefs of the KwaJobe clan who have lived in the area for hundreds of years. The site, which is only accessible to members of the clan who wish to commune with the spirits of their ancestors, may not be visited by the general public. However, a **cultural village** has been established

---

OPPOSITE TOP *A luxurious tented safari camp at Mkuzi Game Reserve is a perfect place from which to experience the night sounds of the African bush.*

OPPOSITE BOTTOM *A water hole at Mkuzi Game Reserve attracts a variety of animals, including zebra, warthog and nyala, and gives visitors the opportunity to watch the animals up close.*

ABOVE *An egret perches atop a pod of hippo wallowing in the waters of Nsumo Pan at Mkuzi Game Reserve.*

Wilderness Trails

Wilderness trails were first introduced to South Africa in what used to be the Umfolozi Game Reserve, now part of the extensive Hluhluwe-Umfolozi Park, in 1959, to give people an opportunity to spend some time in the African bush where they could experience nature at its most pristine.

On a wilderness trail, signs of human intervention are kept to a minimum in order to enhance the wilderness experience. Each trail is designed around the special or characteristic features of its own specific environment and offers unique opportunities for close-up encounters with Africa at its wildest.

Today, the KwaZulu-Natal Nature Conservation Service (KNCS) runs five major wilderness trails, besides the many day walks that are available in most of the reserves. These trails are based in the wilderness zones of Mkuzi and St Lucia game reserves in the Greater St Lucia Wetland Park (*see* page 120), in Hluhluwe-Umfolozi Park (*see* page 108) and in the Drakensberg National Park (*see* page 64).

The trails are generally limited to eight people and need to be booked well in advance. All equipment and provisions are loaded onto donkeys, which then carry the gear to the overnight camps, leaving hikers free to enjoy the scenery. It is possible to spend two, three or four nights in the wilderness areas, depending on what each game reserve offers.

Nothing can beat the exhilaration of waking up to the twittering of birds and rustling of small creatures as they venture through the undergrowth. Early each morning after breakfast, the group sets out from their trail camp in single file, an armed ranger in front and one behind. The distance that is covered every day varies, but generally you should be able to walk about 10 kilometres a day for a period of three consecutive days.

The trails are not get-fit hikes, but rather a good walk during which time the trails ranger will point out anything of interest that you may encounter along the way. This is a most rewarding way of experiencing the bush, as it will make you more aware of your surroundings.

The **Mkuzi Wilderness Trail**, in the Greater St Lucia Wetland Park, is a three-night trail. It winds through magnificent fig forests, past fever tree-lined pans and swamps, and round the foot of the rugged Lebombo Mountains, providing excellent opportunities for seeing both the white and the more elusive black rhino. The hotter parts of the day are spent relaxing at the trails camps, cooling off at a nearby pool or watching game from the hides. The Mkuzi trails season runs from March to November.

Also in the Greater St Lucia Wetland Park is the **St Lucia Wilderness Trail**. Following natural hippo trails for much of the time, trailists explore the dunes and coastal forests of the area, as well as the ever-changing wetlands and grasslands.

One of the highlights of this trail is a canoe trip on Lake St Lucia before heading down to explore the magnificent, seemingly endless beaches north of Cape Vidal. This is a four-night trail: two nights are spent at Bhangazi Tented Camp overlooking the lovely Lake Bhangazi, and the second and third nights are spent in the wilderness on the eastern shores of Lake St Lucia.

close by where members of the community make and sell traditional crafts, such as functional and decorative woodcarvings and basketry.

Accommodation within the reserve is varied. A **caravan park and campsite** are situated adjacent to the Emshopi entrance gate, the **Umkumbi Tented Bush Lodge** is near the Mantuma Main Camp and is situated in the controlled hunting area, the

Nhlonhlela Bush Lodge lies on the edge of the Nhlonhlela Pan, and there are also self-catering bungalows, rest huts and a beautifully situated, self-catering tented camp adjacent to **Mantuma Main Camp**.

Sodwana Bay Park

Sodwana Bay Park is situated on the edge of the Greater St Lucia Wetland Park, and Sodwana Bay lies at its far northern end. Its campsite is busy and popular, mainly because the fishing in the area is excellent – Sodwana has produced record catches of sailfish and billfish – and the beach offers safe ski-boat launching. This is probably one of the closest launch sites to Africa's southernmost offshore coral reefs.

The diversity of fish and invertebrates that can be found on these reefs has made Sodwana Bay one of the most popular

BELOW *The long, sandy beach at Sodwana Bay Park, with Jesser Point in the distance.*

OPPOSITE *A group of scuba divers launching a boat in the waves off the beach at Sodwana Bay, ready to explore the magical underwater world of coral reefs and colourful tropical fish.*

scuba-diving locales in the country. During holiday seasons, the beach is packed with four-wheel-drive vehicles, people picnicking and a proliferation of scuba-diving charter operators. Scuba tanks and wetsuit-clad bodies are everywhere to be seen. Early each morning, ski-boats packed with six to eight divers plunge through the surf and head out to sea to experience life on the coral reefs, deep below in the warm waters of the Indian Ocean. During the months of December and January, depending on the tides, turtle tours are offered in the evenings for camp residents.

Turtle Breeding

Sea turtles are survivors of one of the most ancient reptilian orders, with a fossil history dating back over 200 million years. Once on the brink of extinction along the Tongaland coast, they have slowly been increasing in number. This is largely due to the turtle research project which has been run by the KwaZulu-Natal Nature Conservation Service since 1963. The project, one of the longest-running marine research projects in the world, has been monitoring the breeding of turtles from Sodwana Bay to Kosi Bay.

Loggerhead and leatherback turtles breed along the long, relatively uninhabited stretch of northern KwaZulu-Natal's coastline, and, each night during the breeding season, teams of monitors drive and walk along the beaches looking for these ancient, lumbering beasts. Each turtle is fitted with a tag if she does not already have one, usually on the right front flipper. In an attempt to understand and monitor the turtles' movements better, researchers have in recent years been attaching satellite transponders to the backs of selected turtles, enabling them to track exactly where the turtles go.

Baby loggerhead turtle hatchlings start their arduous journey to the sea having dug out of their nest high up in the sand dunes.

A massive leatherback turtle covers her nest with soft, moist sand after laying her eggs.

A number of tours are run by the KwaZulu-Natal Nature Conservation Service, taking visitors out at night to try to spot these great beasts as they come out of the sea and up into the sand dunes to lay their eggs. Watching the massive leatherbacks and loggerheads in the age-old ritual of digging in the sand with their flippers and flicking it out in slow motion is truly one of the great experiences in this world. Some of the lodges in the Maputaland Coastal Forest Reserve, such as Kosi Forest Lodge and Rocktail Bay Lodge in particular (*see* page 136), can arrange trips with the turtle monitors to see this phenomenon. Later in the season, when the eggs hatch, hundreds of tiny turtle hatchlings emerge from a nest, usually in the dead of night, and wriggle their way down to the water's edge. Sadly, many little hatchlings are snapped up by predatory ghost crabs, and still more by larger fish waiting offshore. However, some do survive and, as adults, return to these selfsame beaches, fortunately protected as a marine reserve, to lay their eggs, season after season.

PHINDA RESOURCE RESERVE

Phinda is cradled in the centre of the vast, ecologically diverse region of Maputaland. On its north-eastern border, Phinda Resource Reserve adjoins Mkuzi Game Reserve, thereby substantially increasing the amount of land in this area which now is under conservation. Traditionally, herds of wild game roamed these hills and plains, but earlier in the century they were used as agricultural land. The Zulu word *phinda* means 'the return' – an appropriate name for the 15 000 hectares of land that was once misused farmlands and which has been painstakingly restored to its rightful heritage. This region is home to no fewer than seven ecosystems and an extraordinary range of wildlife.

Phinda, a 'big five' reserve with a wide range of game, has adopted a progressive approach to the wilderness experience. In addition to outstanding game drives with highly knowledgeable guides, the reserve also offers bush walks, birding safaris and a stunning early-morning or evening sundowner **River Boat Trip** on the Mzinene River where you can enjoy incredible bird-viewing and see hippo and crocodile at close range. It is also possible to board a **Phinda aircraft** in the morning to fly over the spectacular Maputaland wilderness and plains, shimmering pans, the freshwater Lake Sibaya and some of the highest vegetated coastal dune forests in the world. And, if that is not enough, Phinda has expanded their wilderness experience to include the coast, taking guests also by air on an incredible beach adventure to the pristine beaches of Maputaland.

This coastline is home to turtles, ghost crabs, sea birds and a myriad aquatic life, including some 1 200 species of tropical and subtropical fish – closely rivalling Australia's Great Barrier Reef for diversity of species. **Scuba safaris** to Sodwana Bay and **deep-sea fishing expeditions** are also on offer. (In order to promote the conservation of Maputaland's marine life, Phinda encourages a 'tag and release' policy.) Back in the reserve, you can visit the **Zulu Cultural Village** that will give you insight into the traditional lifestyle and customs of Zulu people.

Malaria

Malaria is considered one of the biggest stumbling blocks to tourism development in certain parts of Africa, and is one of the most notorious killers in history. In South Africa, there are a number of areas where visitors should take precautions against being bitten by mosquitoes. Malaria occurs in the far northern regions of KwaZulu-Natal, such as those bordering Mozambique and Swaziland, stretching down as far south as Lake St Lucia.

Transmission of malaria is highest during the warm and wet months – between November and April – when every precaution should be taken to avoid being bitten. As a rule of thumb, there is generally less risk of contracting malaria at altitudes above 1 500 metres.

Malaria is a serious parasitic disease transmitted by an infected, female Anopheles mosquito. When one of these mosquitoes bites a person, it injects malaria parasites into the blood. The parasite, once in the human bloodstream, passes into the liver where it stays for between a week and several months before replicating and sending out more parasites into the blood. The parasites destroy the red blood cells and cause the remaining blood cells to become sticky. The disease propagates when a person already infected is bitten by another mosquito, which in turn becomes infected – and bites someone else.

Although there are four species of mosquito that can infect humans with malaria, only one type of malaria, Plasmodium falciparum, is life-threatening. Factors that encourage the propagation of malaria are high minimum night-time temperatures and a high population of Anopheles mosquitoes, a phenomenon which often occurs following warm, wet periods. The Anopheles mosquito feeds at night to provide itself with enough nutrition before laying eggs, so this is the time to take extra precautions. Apply insect repellents to exposed skin, wear long-sleeved clothing and long pants when outdoors in the evenings, and, at night, use mosquito netting if your bedroom is not air-conditioned. You can also spray insecticide or burn a mosquito coil before going to bed. A variety of anti-malarial prophylactics should also be taken, and note that accurate advice regarding the appropriateness of your medication is vital – as is information about your destination's malarial risk.

LEFT *The luxurious, glassed and beautifully situated accommodation units at Phinda Forest Lodge bring you close to nature, allowing views of animals and birds in the surrounding forest during the day and night.*

OPPOSITE *Phinda Resource Reserve not only gives guests the opportunity to see wild animals in their natural habitat, but also offers excursions to ancient fossil beds which are located in the reserve itself.*

The Phinda lodges are as much part of the overall African experience as are the game and fabulous ecosystems. The four magnificently designed private lodges each have their own theme. **Forest Lodge** consists of 16 stilted, glass chalets that appear to float between the forest floor and the towering torchwood trees. The walls are actually windows onto the forest canopy beyond, which at all times of the day is alive with birds and small creatures, and sometimes even the occasional warthog or antelope can be seen in the undergrowth. **Vlei Lodge**, one of the newest lodges, is also on stilts and also has much glass, but with the addition of thatch and teak. This, and Rock Lodge, evokes the romance of old Africa, and, at night, when the oil lamps are lit, the rooms glow gently against the warm wooden features. Each suite has its own small outdoor deck and private plunge pool. **Mountain Lodge** and **Rock Lodge** are based in the southern section of the reserve. At Mountain Lodge, the spacious split-level suites have private lounges and en-suite bathrooms opening up onto a personal deck with views stretching over the vast bushveld, while at Rock Lodge, the roughly hewn stone and adobe walls of the six suites are built into the rock face looking over the magnificent Leopard Rock.

MAPUTALAND MARINE AND COASTAL FOREST RESERVES

Made up of Kosi Bay, Rocktail Bay, Lake Sibaya and down to Sodwana Bay, the Maputaland Marine and Coastal Forest reserves stretch from Kosi Bay, on the border of Mozambique, to the northern edge of the Greater St Lucia Wetland Park.

Kosi Bay

Although Kosi Bay is a long haul to reach – the access roads are still predominantly gravel and look set to remain that way for some time to come – it is worth the effort to get there. Despite its name, Kosi Bay is an estuary and not a bay at all. It comprises a chain of four freshwater lakes – alive with hippos, crocodiles and a variety of fish – stretching for about 18 kilometres before opening into the sea at Kosi Bay. This is coastal wilderness at its most magical.

The area is still sparsely developed, and if you are planning a visit, camping or caravanning are your main accommodation options. But for something more luxurious, you can try **Kosi Bay Lodge** or the more upmarket **Kosi Forest Lodge**, which is

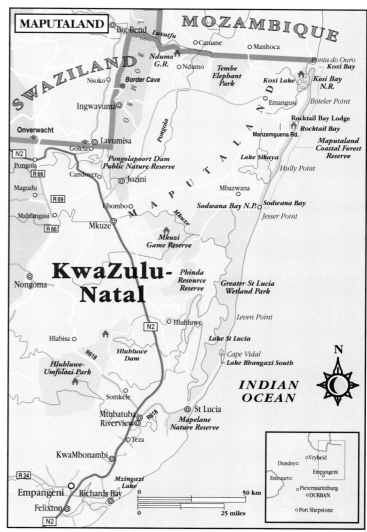

The Traditional *Fonya*

One of the most fascinating things to see in Maputaland is a traditional *fonya*, or fish drive. A number of pans are found in the region, some of which dry up completely during the winter months and start to fill again in the rainy summer season. In the old days, usually during the winter months or when water levels were low, the local men would get together and, armed with spears and the distinctive *fonya* baskets, head for the pans. A group would start at one end of the pan and, in a long row, 'beat' or chase the fish across the pan. When a shoal of fish was isolated, the baskets were used to trap them. The hole at the top of the *fonya* basket is useful because a person can grab or stab the fish with a spear while it is trapped in the basket.

These days, it is mainly the women who carry out a fish drive. It is a noisy and happy social occasion in which the whole community joins in. You may find it difficult to see a *fonya* because it happens, as the locals say, 'when the time is right', which could be any time. However, if you are in the area and would like to participate in this fascinating ritual, you should speak to the locals – and, if a drive is about to take place, make an effort to go along. You will not be disappointed. The beautiful *fonya* baskets have become very popular with tourists and can often be bought at roadside craft stalls.

Kosi Bay Community Camp

This small camp was established by the three communities (the nKovokheni, KwaDapha and eMalangeni) who live on the peninsula that divides the Kosi lakes from the sea. These communities resisted attempts to be forcibly removed from their ancestral land when it was proclaimed a nature reserve. The Kosi Bay Community Camp centres around a large shack which was built and used by the late David Webster, an anthropologist who worked in the area but who was murdered at his home in Johannesburg by members of the notorious apartheid hit squads in the late 1980s.

The original idea behind establishing the tourist camp was that, if it were successful, there would be less chance that the communities would be moved. Through the community camp, you can arrange to visit one of the nearby families, have a meal with them, drink some ilala wine and listen to the intriguing stories of their lives.

The camp is situated on one of the most beautiful peninsulas in the country. On one side are pristine indigenous dune forests and the magnificent Kosi lakes with their crystal-clear waters,

BELOW *Thonga fishermen at Kosi Bay lure their fish into specially constructed traps where they are easier to spear.*

RIGHT *The ancient fish traps of Kosi Bay have been maintained by many generations of Thonga people.*

wonderfully private and romantic; both lie close to the lake system. A community camp lies on the peninsula that forms the barrier between the sea and the freshwater lakes.

Kosi Forest Lodge is not situated close to the beach, but a short drive and a short walk past a magnificent stand of giant raffia palms (still harvested by locals) will get you onto one of the lakes from where lodge staff take small motorised boat trips to the ancient fish traps (*see* page 135) on the estuary. Kosi Forest Lodge also runs one of the nicest 'ilala palm wine tours', on request (*see* page 136).

and, on the other side, the warm Indian Ocean and long unspoilt beaches stretch for miles. This is where turtles breed, where ghost crabs scuttle in the night, and where the translucent water provides unrivalled snorkelling.

These communities are the ancestral owners of the ancient fish traps and who, to this day, continue the age-old rituals of clearing the fish traps to feed their families. Others have been trained as turtle tour guides. But, for the most part, the people live in this paradise of Maputaland in much the same way as their ancestors did before them.

The Ancient Kosi Fish Traps

Zulu people are more often associated with their Nguni cattle and are not well known as fishermen, but the Thonga people of Maputaland are excellent and knowledgeable fishermen. In **Makhawulani,** the first of Kosi's lakes closest to the mouth, are situated ancient fish 'kraals' or fish traps that have been built and maintained by generations of local people. It is thought that some of the fish traps possibly date back to prehistoric times. Most of them are very old – few new ones have ever been established – and they are generally handed down and maintained by a single family for generations.

The wooden fish kraals are almost sculptural in shape, and are carefully positioned in the beautiful clear waters of the estuary. They consist of a fence of thin poles, woven with reeds, which is placed in the water in such a way that the larger fish are guided into the circular kraal and trapped there. The smaller fish can slip out through the gaps, making this an environmentally friendly manner of fishing. The fishermen check their traps at certain times of the day and spear or catch by hand any fish caught inside.

The only sensible way for visitors to see the fish traps up close is by boat. The traps are usually cleared on a daily basis, and, if you do not have your own boat, it is possible to join a guided

135

tour, run regularly by the lodges. If you are there at the right time of day, you may be lucky enough to see a fisherman knee-deep in the water clearing his traps.

Raffia Palms and Ilala Palm Wine

The coastal belt of Maputaland is one of the few areas in the country where the massive and majestic raffia palm grows – although there are not as many stands of this plant as there once were.

In the past, the raffia used to be the prime source of roofing material in the area. Nowadays corrugated iron is used, and although it may not look as pretty, it certainly takes the pressure off the few remaining palm stands. The presence of raffia palms means that there is every chance of seeing the rare **palmnut vulture**, a bird which is thought to be almost entirely dependent on the raffia for survival.

Another very useful palm found growing in the area, and one on which people rely heavily, is the ilala palm. Its fronds are used for making domestic handicrafts and it is from this palm that ilala palm wine is made. Ilala wine is synonymous with Maputaland and, although painstakingly labour intensive, it is a growing industry.

The tapping of *ubusulu,* or ilala palm wine, was once the business of men, but, with more men going to work in the cities, the work has fallen increasingly on women.

A healthy clump of ilala palm is selected, burnt and, some time later, the stem trimmed. A funnel-shaped leaf is inserted into the stem. The sap then drips into a calabash, tin or bottle. The plant is trimmed about three times a day over a period of five to seven weeks. The sap does not need time to ferment as it is alcoholic right away, but it does become stronger the longer it is left. It is a good source of vitamins and has played an important part in the diet of the locals. When visiting any of the Thonga people, it is likely that you will be offered palm wine, but be warned: it may look like litchi juice and taste sweet and refreshing, but it should be drunk with caution.

Rocktail Bay Lodge

Tucked away in the Maputaland Coastal Forest Reserve, midway between Kosi Bay and Sodwana Bay, is Rocktail Bay Lodge, situated in coastal dune forest behind a great dune. A boardwalk trail leads down to a beautiful, pristine beach where you will seldom see another person for miles in either direction.

This special lodge is run along the same lines as any game lodge, except that it is a beach lodge, and apart from hippo in the nearby pans, the odd little antelope in the dune forests, the surrounding grasslands and some beautiful birds, there is not much game to see. But one of the many highlights of staying at the lodge is that, during the turtle season, you can join the staff when they drive along the beaches in a four-wheel-drive vehicle to monitor turtles at night. Rocktail Bay Lodge is contributing significantly to the running of the turtle breeding research

BOTTOM LEFT *The raffia palms in the far northern coastal regions are essential for the existence of the rare palmnut vulture.*

BELOW *The luxurious tree-house accommodation at Rocktail Bay Lodge is situated in the indigenous coastal dune forests which separate the interior from the long, empty beaches of the Maputaland coast.*

OPPOSITE TOP *Dinner at Rocktail Bay Lodge is usually a sociable affair out under the trees.*

OPPOSITE BOTTOM *The freshwater lake system of Lake Sibaya is home to crocodile, hippo and a variety of water birds.*

project which has been taking place along this stretch of coast for a few decades, providing a unique opportunity to see one of the wonders of nature.

Other leisure activities offered at the lodge include snorkelling, scuba-diving and saltwater fly-fishing. Guests are driven, with cooler boxes filled with iced drinks, to Black Rock or any one of the smaller secluded beaches where the water is crystal clear, ideal for swimming and snorkelling, and where the fishing is good.

Lake Sibaya

A short distance south of Rocktail Bay lies Lake Sibaya which at 7 750 ha is the country's largest freshwater lake. It is similar to but smaller than the necklace of lakes at Kosi Bay. It is also easily as beautiful and unspoilt, with great coastal dune forests looming as a backdrop between the fresh water and the sea.

A road runs around the edge of the lake for which a four-wheel-drive vehicle and a permit are needed (the permit can be obtained at the gate into the reserve area). Part of the road runs through long stretches of coastal dune forest humming with cicadas, and later it runs right onto the lip of the lake, from where it is likely that you will see crocodile or hippopotamus. It is a breathtaking sight to witness an African sunset from the edge of the lake, with a hippo trundling out of the water to feed in the nearby reeds and fish eagle calling overhead.

TEMBE ELEPHANT RESERVE

Tembe, the third-largest game reserve in KwaZulu-Natal, is situated in Maputaland in the north-eastern region of the province, adjoining the Mozambique border. Tembe is unique in a number of ways, one of them being that it is the home to the province's biggest indigenous elephant herd. At one time, these elephants were the last remaining free-ranging herd in South Africa, moving seasonally between Mozambique and Maputaland. These magnificent beasts are Tembe's main attraction and signs of them are everywhere in its sand forest, grasslands, swamps and woodlands. A number of well-placed hides allow you to observe these amazing animals at close quarters.

But elephant is not all you will see at the water holes and in the bush as Tembe boasts four of the 'big five' (leopard, rhino, buffalo and elephant). On a game drive or from a discreet hide, you could see black or white rhino, buffalo, hippo, giraffe, nyala, kudu and a diversity of other small mammals. If you are very lucky, you could even see leopard.

An animal which you are unlikely to see as easily anywhere else, is Africa's tiniest antelope, the shy little suni with its wagging tail.

Tembe Safari Camp, a small, exclusive tented camp tucked into the sand forest, is the only accommodation available in the reserve. The staff are knowledgeable about birds and plants and

ABOVE *Elephant are a daily sighting at Tembe Elephant Reserve, where visitors can also see leopard, rhino and buffalo as well as many of the smaller game species.*

RIGHT *The open decks of Wilderness Safari's luxury bush camp at Ndumo Game Reserve look out over one of the many pans in the reserve.*

OPPOSITE TOP *Giraffe are often spotted under the fever trees at Nyamiti Pan in Ndumo Game Reserve.*

OPPOSITE BOTTOM *Hiking at Shokwe Pan in Ndumo Game Reserve takes visitors through the amazing and beautiful fig tree forest.*

will give good advice as to where best to spot animals. Day and night game drives are offered, and to come across a massive elephant bull silhouetted in the moonlight is an exhilarating experience. Only a limited number of daily permits are issued for entrance into Tembe Elephant Reserve, so you will need to make enquiries before planning your visit.

NDUMO GAME RESERVE

Also on the Mozambique border but further west than Tembe is Ndumo Game Reserve. Possibly one of the premier bird-watching reserves in the country, Ndumo boasts more than 400 species of bird. During the summer months, or between October and April when the Banzi and Nyamiti pans start to fill up, the birding is outstanding as the summer migrants take up residence. Surrounded by giant sycamore figs and the almost luminous green-yellow fever trees, the beautiful pans also draw large numbers of water birds, hippos and crocodiles, which are a feature of the reserve. Fish eagles call out across the pans and black egrets, pygmy geese, white-faced ducks and jacanas can be seen paddling in the water or high-stepping over lily pads. Crested guineafowl and Pel's fishing owl are rare birds that can be seen here.

Maputaland – Wilderness Wonderland

ABOVE *The strange, eerie, pale-green fever trees that are so characteristic of Ndumo Game Reserve are seen here on the edge of Nyamiti Pan. Giant sycamore figs are also fairly common in the reserve, especially around the pans.*

OPPOSITE TOP *The delightful little African jacana nips along the water's surface on giant lily pads in the tranquil water pans of Ndumo Game Reserve.*

Instead of driving around the reserve on your own, a good idea is to join a guided game drive. Going around the reserve with someone who knows the area, the animals and the birds can be a very rewarding experience.

No camping is allowed in this reserve, but there is the small, reasonably priced **Ndumo Hutted Camp** which is run by the KwaZulu-Natal Nature Conservation Service. **Wilderness Safaris,** one of the country's premier private safari operators, has

established a small, luxury tented camp on the edge of one of the big pans which characterise Ndumo. **Ndumo Wilderness Camp** – luxurious East African safari-style tents each with their own bathroom and veranda overlooking Banzi Pan – is perched on wooden stilts with decks extending over the water where you can sit and enjoy the animals coming down to drink.

USEFUL INFORMATION

Note that bookings for provincial reserve campsites can be made via the officers in charge of the various reserves; other accommodation must be booked through the KwaZulu-Natal Nature Conservation Service head office.

Cape Vidal: Private Bag X04, St Lucia Estuary, 3936, tel. (035) 590-9012
Charter's Creek: PO Box 1597, Mtubatuba, 3935, tel. (035) 550-9000
Crocodile Centre: 3 kilometres outside St Lucia village, tel. (035) 590-1386
False Bay Park: PO Box 222, Hluhluwe, 3960, tel. (035) 562-0061
Fanie's Island: PO Box 1259, Mtubatuba, 3930, tel. (035) 550-9035
Kosi Bay Lodge: Book through Wilderness Safaris (*see* below)
Kosi Forest Lodge: PO Box 1593, Eshowe, 3815, tel. (035) 474-1504, fax (035) 474-1490, email: isibindi@iafrica.com
KwaZulu-Natal Nature Conservation Service: PO Box 1306, Cascades, 3202. tel. (033) 845-1000, fax (033) 845-1001, e-mail: bookings@rhino.org.za
KwaZulu-Natal Tourism: tel. (031) 304-7144, fax (031) 305-6693, e-mail: tkzn@iafrica.com
Mapelane Nature Reserve: Private Bag X01, St Lucia, 3936, tel. (035) 590-1407
Mkuzi Game Reserve: Private Bag X550, Mkuze, 3965, tel. (035) 573-0003
Ndumo Game Reserve: Private Bag X356, KwaNgwanase, 3973, tel. (035) 591-0032
Ndumo Wilderness Camp: Book through Wilderness Safaris (*see* below)
Phinda Resource Reserve: Private Bag X6001, Hluhluwe, 3960, tel. (035) 571-0600. For reservations, contact: Conservation Corporation, tel. (011) 784-7077, fax (011) 784-7667, email: reservations@conscorp.co.za
Rocktail Bay: Book through Wilderness Safaris (*see* below)
Sodwana Bay Park: Private Bag X310, Mbazwana, 3974, tel. (035) 571-0051
St Lucia Publicity Association: PO Box 299, St Lucia, 3936, tel. (035) 590-1075
Wilderness Safaris: PO Box 5219, Rivonia, 2128, tel. (011) 883-0747, fax (011) 883-0911, email: enquiry@wilderness.co.za

INDEX

Index